Your Mess Is NOT Your Message

Branding Strategies for Solopreneurs

by Cathy Goodwin, Ph.D.

Your Mess Is NOT Your Message

Branding Strategies for Solopreneurs

ISBN 978-1-7324400-3-6

Library of Congress Control Number: 2024924398

Your Mess Is NOT Your Message

Branding Strategies for Solopreneurs

by Cathy Goodwin, PH.D.

Contents

A Better Way to Brand for Solopreneurs Forward by Alex Hillman

If you're a solopreneur, you've probably heard advice along the lines of "*you are the brand.*"

And while that's true in a sense, the way most people use this advice to approach their branding is all wrong. This is especially true for one-person service-based businesses who routinely waste time on branding before they've even worked with a client, let alone delivered results!

In fact, this problem is so pervasive that it was one of the first lessons in my book *The Tiny MBA*, where I confront readers with two common branding mistakes:

> *Branding can be valuable for your business, but creating a brand is not a first step for starting a business. It's not even one of the first 200 steps.*

and

> *Most people confuse "brand" with "marketing." "Marketing" is a wide range of activities which help people believe that you understand them. "Brand" is the result of doing that right.*

Whether you've heard my lessons before, or you're reading them here for the first time, I want you to keep them in mind as you read the rest of this book!

Too often, new entrepreneurs and solopreneurs especially get caught up in the wrong kinds of branding advice. When they tell their story, they overshare personal struggles in a bid for connection.

But your clients don't care about your mess. They care about what you can do for *them*. These tactics might grab attention, but they rarely build the kind of trust and connection that leads to long-term business success.

That's where Cathy's approach in *Your Mess Is Not Your Message* really shines. She flips everything around to focus on understanding your *client's* backstory, and crafting a story that resonates with them while showcasing your expertise. You'll find through the examples ahead that this approach feels a lot more honest and practical...and by the end you'll understand *why* this approach works better, too!

At the heart of Cathy's strategy are **the five "story archetypes"**: The Role Model, The Innovator, The Educator, The Passionate Advocate, and The Celebrity. Each archetype represents a unique way you can relate to your audience through storytelling, helping you find the approach that feels the most natural for you and your clients while also suggesting the most common pitfalls to avoid.

Cathy backs each one up with real-world examples of solopreneurs who have embraced their archetype and built thriving, authentic brands.

In *Your Mess Is Not Your Message*, Cathy walks you through each of these five archetypes, showing how to use storytelling, content creation, and email marketing to grow your business.

So get ready to learn:

- The truth about why traditional branding advice often fails solopreneurs, and how to avoid those pitfalls.

- How to identify *your* dominant story archetype, and craft a brand narrative that's authentic to you.

- A bunch of practical strategies for using storytelling, content, and email marketing to attract and retain clients.

This book is a practical guide for solopreneurs who are tired of trying to fit into a mold that doesn't work. Cathy's tough-love approach will help you rethink branding and focus on what really matters: delivering results, building relationships, and letting your brand evolve naturally.

Follow Cathy's frameworks to create the foundation of a brand that you can use *today*, and build on as your business grows over time!

To your success,

Alex Hillman
Co-founder of *Indy Hall* and *Stacking the Bricks*
Author of *The Tiny MBA*

Introduction
The new solopreneurs and the new world of marketing

Many years ago, the only people who used the Internet were members of a few elite universities or secret government agencies.

I was thinking about starting a business. A career consultant told me firmly, "Nobody will hire you unless they meet you in person first. You'll have to incorporate facetime in your model."

Today, I regularly find money in my account from people I've never met. I see their names when they come through on my payment processor. They don't even bother to call or text. They might not even be in the United States.

They go to my website. They like what they see and run their credit cards for amounts ranging from $27 for an ebook to $350 for a consultation program.

I'm a solopreneur.

Working as a one-person service-based business, getting clients remotely, I'm one of an army of solopreneurs. The term remains unfamiliar to many mainstream marketers, although we number in the millions and we're the fastest-growing component in the business sector.

The US Chamber of Commerce website[1] says, "A solopreneur works independently and doesn't hire employees or other team members.

Solopreneurs often run service-based businesses, like freelancing, consulting, or web development."

Solopreneurs are not choosing big Madison Avenue agencies.

When they turn to marketing, solopreneurs can't follow the Madison Avenue model. People don't buy our services from watching television ads. Sometimes they decide to buy while they're on our websites for the very first time. Maybe for the first time.

That means a solopreneur's marketing works differently from the brands of the big beer companies, or the sportswear company with the big swish. It's completely different from what I used to teach as a college professor in my Marketing 101 classes.

Marketing When The Brand Is YOU

The most important - and noticeable - difference is that the brand is YOU for a solopreneur. You're not selling chemicals in water, like a beer company. You're selling yourself. That means you must promote yourself as an expert without sounding like a conceited jerk. And you don't have a lot of helpful guidance.

I discovered this myself when I was a new solopreneur.. My first website focused on midlife career change. It's still up, and I get an occasional client now and then.

While learning to market that site, I took a copywriting course from a brand-new copywriter…and got hooked. I've always been a writer, so this step felt natural.

This time around I knew just enough about marketing to be dangerous. When I first set up shop online as a copywriter, I branded my business "Copy-Cat Copywriting." A publicist had named her business The Publicity Hound so I thought…why not?

Many experienced marketers loved the name. It was clever and catchy, they said.

For instance, I met a high-powered "branding expert" at a networking event. He got excited about the concept. He suggested taking it further, with "purr-fect copy" and other feline attributes. In fact, for a mere $5000 he'd help me polish the brand to perfection.

Fortunately, I resisted the temptation.

Looking back now, I realize the brand did nothing to create realistic, desirable expectations. It was Madison Avenue branding applied to me, a solopreneur. And it didn't work.

In fact, "copy-cat" is just the opposite of what I was doing. I'm an original. I abhor cookie-cutter marketing. People who know me usually sigh and say, "Well, Cathy, you're … different." That's when they're being nice.

Ironically, I had a perfectly good story. On my website, I wrote about business owners who were so afraid of sounding sales-y that they went to the other extreme. They wrote timid copy that tiptoed around the edges of their benefits.

I should have paid more attention to that story.

That was only the beginning of the bad advice I received. Another 'branding expert" suggested branding on my energy and enthusiasm. She suggested using images of coffee to create a memorable persona. No problem: I could have Coffee Pot consultations and Cappuccino workshops.

Since then, I've seen many other entrepreneurs who brand themselves based on personal qualities, including "caffeinated," "rebel," and "curly-haired."

I've also met business owners who went to the opposite extreme. They attended webinars sponsored by large agencies. They were encouraged to learn from the beer companies, the cola companies, and the sportswear companies.

"If it worked for them," they were told, "it should work for you too!"

More recently, we began to hear about branding with a story.

At first, that made sense to me. As a copywriter, I'd been encouraging my clients to share their stories before I wrote any content. I would learn a lot about the company from the stories they told.

Along the way, though, I learned that many people were spinning marketing advice out of air. They knew even less than I did. They made things up. They sounded pretty good, too.

I was building my brand and working with solopreneur clients ranging from attorneys to astrologers, with many consultants and coaches in between. And they had no place to go for help.

We were supposed to show our clients we were human. We were supposed to be "vulnerable." We were supposed to share mistakes, flaws, and darkest moments.

In particular, marketers encouraged small businesses to share a "hero's journey" story. That was supposed to be a story about how you found a problem, struggled, and eventually found success. Clients were supposed to be inspired by your success. After all, you walked in their shoes.

Some branding consultants even borrowed the slogan, "Your mess is your message."

Alas, all too many hard-working, purpose-driven solopreneurs took this slogan to heart. They shared stories of difficult childhoods, growing up on welfare, or experiencing physical and mental breakdowns. The word "cringeworthy" was invented to describe some of those stories.

A lot of people don't have rags-to-riches stories. They opened their businesses with a stash of cash and never looked back. They live happy, well-balanced lives.

But some business owners want to share, "I'm like you. I've made mistakes."

That may be fine if you're a successful life coach. But if you're a criminal defense lawyer, you probably didn't walk in your client's shoes. If you did, you'd have trouble getting approved to practice law.

As I often say, "You don't have to have a heart attack to be a good cardiologist."

One of my clients told me, "I went to a live event with a big-name marketer. He told us to share our darkest stories. We should make one up if we don't have a horror story."

After all, he said, Brene Brown tells us to be vulnerable.

Really? Was this the same Brene Brown I read?

Brene Brown never told anybody to give up their boundaries. She never told anyone to share personal stories with strangers, let alone their prospective clients.

I studied a lot of psychology in graduate school. The slogan "Your mess is your message" comes from clinical psychology. If you've got a lot of problems, you're getting a message to make some changes. You don't share your problems with your clients.

Even if you don't have a mess, we're often advised to "let people connect with you as a person." Let your audience get closer as they learn more about your personal life.

Many business owners have done this successfully. They talk about gardening, children, and cooking. They share details of their family life.

Alas, not everyone has stories to share. Some people are single with no children. Some live with one cat. I'm here to tell you, you can only go so far with cat videos before your audience decides you're too weird to be trusted -- even if they're cat people themselves.

Some people created "normal" personas for their stories. They invented nieces and nephews when they had no brothers and sisters. They invented grandchildren. So much for authenticity.

I got into trouble when I tried to be more personal. I live in a large city, so I rely on public transportation. I take a lot of buses. In Philadelphia that can be faster than driving. Yet when I shared anecdotes about my day, my readers thought I must be destitute. Didn't I have a car?

I never tried to explain why I chose a small apartment because it's blissfully quiet 24/7. You'll never understand if you haven't lived in an urban condo.

Most importantly, I noticed a curious phenomenon. A story that worked for one business owner would backfire for another solopreneur in the same industry.

I admired a business coach I'll write about later, Cindy Bidar[2]. She shares all kinds of delightful, home-y stories about everyday life

Then there's another business coach, Connie Ragen Green, who's built an online empire by sharing stories of her personal life. I admired her too.

But then we had other solopreneurs in the same field who rarely shared personal stories. Some shared only stories about their clients' success; if they had spouses and families, we never heard about them. Others shared bits of stories to illustrate points they wanted to make about business.

Those who shared personal stories had developed guidelines about what they would and wouldn't share. They cultivated their brand.

What made the difference?

If you're a solopreneur, your brand is built on storytelling. Every story you tell will become part of your brand (even that casual story about showing up somewhere with mismatched socks). You never know what story will get burned into your audience's brain.

So for business, we can forget about storytelling as a creative act. A business owner isn't writing a movie script (unless she's a videographer, but that's another...story). You use your story strategically. Each story has a purpose, such as branding, selling, or explaining what you offer.

Even more important, each story you tell and every piece of content you create must contribute to building your brand.

That's why a business coach like Cindy will share one type of story. Another business coach will never tell personal stories the way Cindy does; she talks about how her clients benefited from her unique process. Still another uses stories to explain concepts; he might share a family anecdote, but only when the story makes the concept easier to understand.

As I worked with clients and studied the most successful solopreneurs, I found their brands and stories fit into five categories, which I call their story archetypes.

These business owners had never considered their marketing or branding in terms of these archetypes. Unconsciously, they had adopted the qualities of their archetype and applied them consistently. They reflected their archetype in the content they created, the stories they told, their marketing approach…even the way they signed off on their emails.

Business owners resonated with the idea. Newer solopreneurs found archetypes an easy path to branding, simplifying their marketing.

Archetypes give you a framework that goes beyond branding on personality quirks but doesn't require you to think like a cola or beer company. They're designed for service-based solopreneurs, not big brands with big agencies, big budgets, and big television commercials.

Sometimes I get asked, "What's the archetype for this soft drink? This airline?"

I have to say, "I have no idea. They don't need me. The solopreneurs do."

This book grew out of my experience with clients, as a copywriter, strategist, and storyteller.

I've made presentations to diverse audiences, written countless articles, developed self-study courses and held hundreds of one-on-one consultations.

The response has been consistently positive. Successful solopreneurs resonated with the archetype I assigned them: "It feels like me," they'd say.

New solopreneurs get it. They're relieved they don't have to make up stories about how they suffered. They know how to position themselves as they create content and write copy.

Mostly, business owners struggle to find a brand. I like to say, "Once you've got your archetype, finding your brand is like water rolling downhill."

Solopreneur marketing is all about content. Content flows from your stories. Your stories flow from your archetype. Find your archetype, and the rest is the fun part. The fun part is the reason you started your business anyway, right?

Section 1
Branding as YOU is a balancing act

Small business branding is like a balancing act.

First, you have to recognize that you–the business owner–are the brand. Second, you have to recognize that you are a business.

It's now commonplace to recognize that personal branding is a part of many kinds of careers.

Entertainers like Oprah and Ellen Degeneres have been branded as personalities. We know them beyond their most recent network shows.

Sports figures get royalties for their images and jerseys–their own, not the team's. They get known as individuals as they move from team to team.

In Chapter 1, I talk about a scientist who thinks researchers should consider personal branding. They move across laboratories and universities, based on their own personal reputation.

Corporate business executives also brand themselves, sometimes hiring a specialist to do the publicity for them..

In Section 1, I argue that solopreneurs need their own strategy too…but theirs is more of a balancing act. They provide the service as people, but they also come with a business.

So as a solopreneur, you strike a balance between being personal and being a company providing a service.

That means you have to balance between going too small or too large.

Many business owners make the mistake of going too large. When they studied branding in school, they focused on the big brands–the cola drinks, beer companies, sportswear and more.

Many branding seminars designed for small businesses encourage solopreneurs to emulate these big companies. However, when you're selling yourself, you're not giving a personality to chemicals in water: you already have a personality.

Even worse, a lot of marketing coaches encourage solopreneurs to go to the other extreme. So we see many campaigns that gave this book its title. Business owners are encouraged to be "vulnerable" and share stories of hardship.

We also see people branded as "the blond marketer" or "the curly-haired coach." More recently, we're seeing solopreneurs brand themselves as "badass" or "maverick."

Ideally solopreneurs end up with what I call "Middle Bear Branding." The beer brands are too big: they focus on the product and not the person. The personal brands are too small: they focus on the person rather than the service, and they ignore the target market.

The balance will be different for each company. Some solopreneurs brand personal quirks and do very well. Others brand only on the quality of services they provide and the audience's reaction.

Chapter 1:
Why small businesses need their own branding strategy.

What it means to say YOU are the brand.

Peter Hotez[3] is an American physician and researcher. A few years ago, he made a radical suggestion: scientists need to consider personal branding.

At first, the idea seems strange. When you search YouTube for "images of scientists," you find serious-looking people peering into microscopes. Their world seems governed by statistics, not self-promotion.

On the other hand, we've gotten used to the idea of branding individual people. They may or may not be part of someone else's company, but they are their own brand.

Top athletes inevitably become a brand. When Dwight Howard was traded to the Houston Rockets from the Lakers, Kobe Bryant (then the Lakers star player), said, "You have to make decisions that you feel are best for you, best for your family, and *best for your brand*, whatever it may be."

But, scientists?

Hotez points out that few scientists remain at one facility for their entire lives. Every academic research organization wants to hire a "rockstar." Each scientist resembles an entrepreneur, hired based on individual reputation.

"For me," Hoetz says, "the essential elements to cultivate a brand [for scientists] include a self-awareness of who you are, what you wish to project to the public, and, most importantly, what major problem you want to solve."

That's the same recipe for solopreneurs and small business owners who want to brand themselves in a crowded marketplace. Like scientists, they want to be taken seriously and valued for their expertise.

When you're in a business where YOU are the brand, your marketing is based on three principles.

(1) You sell yourself, not an imaginary persona.

Beer companies? Cola drinks? They're selling chemicals in water. Sportswear companies? They're selling fabric.

These consumer brands have to create a personality for their products. That's why you see commercials with adorable puppies and athletes on the edge of a mountain.

You, on the other hand, have a real personality, based on the way you work with clients and deliver your services. You are branded by your story.

You're Charlotte, the money coach who helped her client go from "broke with a lousy credit score" to "proud homeowner who's on track to enjoy a Hawaii vacation."

You're John, the marketing coach who's analyzed exactly "what it takes to get clients through email marketing."

You're Laura, a former schoolteacher who taught herself marketing and now helps others do the same.

You're Lydia the bridal consultant who drove two hours to replace the flowers that wilted on the bride's big day.

You're Joe, who grew up on welfare, built a designer business, and now gets $400 haircuts while living in Beverly Hills.

You're Vincent, the DUI lawyer who spent many hours discovering your client wasn't anywhere near the accident, let alone under the influence of anything.

(2) Every story you tell becomes part of your brand.

The good news is, those blog posts, articles, and interviews all tell a story. People absorb your content. You're branded with your story

But there's a downside to having so much publicity. It's easy to share a story that brands you the wrong way. That's why it's so dangerous to listen to advice like, "Be vulnerable! Share your dark side!"

A business owner I'll call Daniel took this advice to heart. I came across a podcast where he said, "I'm supposed to be more human. My coaches told me to open up." He launched into a story of sliding into a deep, dark depression.

Daniel is now branded as "the guy who had a depressive episode." If he were a life coach, that brand might help him. But he's a business consultant. At best, his clients don't care.

At worst, some will feel uncomfortable when they think of hiring him. After all, he could go off the rails any moment.

Storytelling can't be accidental in this environment. You can't afford to tell a story that doesn't support your strategy.

(3) Buyers often decide to buy while they're actively reading your content.

Why does a big beer company show heart-warming stories of adorable puppies on Superbowl Sunday?

They're creating mental associations. Next time you're in a store or seated at a bar, you will (consciously or unconsciously) get the warm fuzzies and buy the brand.

Your clients don't buy your services this way. They won't come across your services in a grocery store or online listing and associate your name with cute puppies. They search for you online or encounter you in their inboxes.

Therefore being "memorable" becomes less important. When they need help they'll begin the search process. You might have a database of subscribers, but there are no guarantees.

Small Business Branding Is About Being The Middle Bear

When I work on branding with solopreneurs, I keep thinking of Goldilocks and the Three Bears.

Some business owners go too big. They try to follow the examples of the big brands. Then they tell me, "I can't see the point of branding."

I once met a business coach who dismissed the whole topic in two words: "Brand? Schmand."

That's because the big brand style doesn't do anything for them. They share dramatic stories and make beautiful, expensive scripted videos, designed to be seen once and remembered forever.

On the other hand, some solopreneurs go too small. They brand the owner's personality quirks. I've seen people try to brand themselves based upon their hair ("the curly-haired coach" or "the blond designer" or "the intuitive counselor").

Some give themselves out-of-the-box attributes, like "The Rebel Consultant" or "The Maverick Designer."

Worst of all: the "think small" crowd buys into the advice, "Your mess is your message."

I shudder every time someone says that, usually with conviction and sincerity.

As I said in the Introduction, that advice was never intended for marketing. It certainly wasn't intended as a branding strategy.

What happens when people share their messes?

We saw this with Daniel in the example above. At best, their audiences respond with a "Who cares?" shrug. At worst, the business owner gets viewed as a helpless victim. You're "the person with the mess," not "the business that helps me solve my problem."

Prospective clients wonder, "If they're so screwed up, how can they help me?"

Occasionally I've had a client say, "I feel I need to tell this story." I want to respond, "Share your story with a trusted friend. Share with your therapist. For your client, tell a branding story."

Small businesses need Middle Bear Branding: not too big or too small, not too enthusiastic or too humble, but just right. Your brand is about you...but it's you-as-a-business, not you-as-a-person. You'll learn more about these differences in the next chapter.

But first, let's see why it's so easy to go off the rails.

Chapter 2: Your brand will be smaller than the beer guys

Several years ago, I was headed over to the Rittenhouse Square section of Philadelphia to run a few errands before my dance class at the gym. It would normally be a quick trip, but the street I needed was blocked off.

This happens a lot in Philly. Streets are usually blocked off for construction. But this time, the word was out: "The Clydesdales are coming!"

Sure enough, at the very moment when dinner time and happy hours come together, the big brown horses came marching down Walnut Street, looking as if they'd rather be back on the farm. (I know nothing about horses, so I may be reading something into their expressions, if horses can be said to have expressions.)

And even though I'm not much of a beer drinker, I knew exactly what was going on. I've watched their doggy Superbowl commercials more than once.

This beer company's branding is legendary. As soon as we saw the word "Clydesdales," we Philadelphians knew exactly what was going on.

Beer companies tell stories to build brand associations

The Budweiser "adopted dog" ad ran on Super Bowl XLVIII. You can watch it here[4] (if it hasn't been taken down)..

Personally, I love that video. I've watched it many times.

The "adopted dog" story isn't about beer at all. It reinforces the association of "beer" with "cute puppies."

Some "adopted dog" stories also include the Clydesdales.

You watch that cute dog story. You go to the beer store. You see Budweiser cans. You consciously or unconsciously think, "Lost dog."

If the commercial works, you recapture that warm and fuzzy feeling as you look at those beer cans. Who can resist?

What You Can Learn From Big Brands When the Brand is YOU

In an Entrepreneurial Magazine article[5], The Basics of Branding, writer John Williams says, "Your brand is your promise."

Building a brand adds equity to your offer, "which means the added value brought to your company's products or services that allows you to charge more for your brand than what identical, unbranded products command."

As a small business, you too can deliver a credible promise. You can send a message that you're a high-end service: you won't be cheap but you'll deliver quality. You can communicate with consistency

These elements go together. High-end services need to deliver a strong, believable promise. Consistency leads to credibility. And a strong promise makes it easier to be consistent.

You aim for these goals whether you're a big brand or a solopreneur. But you do it differently.

What You Can't Learn From Big Brands

(1) Clients search for you. You rarely get in front of clients to communicate your message over and over.

Cadbury Chocolates created an iconic ad[6] in 2007 featuring a gorilla playing the drums. An article in Contently.com[7] explains how this very successful ad works.

As audiences watch the ad on television, their brains begin working to understand what they see. When the candy bar appears, we have a "branding moment," putting together the story and the product. When we see the Cadbury product in a store, we associate the emotion with the product.

These ads appear in front of shoppers, first as ads, then in a store, whether virtual or brick and mortar.

This style of marketing dates back to the Mad Men era. Ads appeared in front of customers (known as "consumers" in the world of marketing theory). You couldn't escape those ads on television, magazines and newspapers.

Ad-free cable television wasn't invented yet. Neither was social media.

The ads were reinforced when you entered a retail store. You might stand in front of the candy section. You might even notice a large cardboard cutout the manufacturer had created. You'd get the warm fuzzy feeling from the association.

When you promote your services you most likely won't be in anybody's face.

Here in Philadelphia we occasionally see ads for dog walkers tacked to a telephone pole. Health care clinics and universities paint their ads all over our buses. Billboards interrupt our journeys on the highways in and out of the city.

Most solopreneurs work in fields where this kind of advertising makes no sense. Many of us are working online where we rarely get in front of prospective clients. They have to search for us.

Some prospective clients find you, your blog, or your landing page after searching online. Your website comes up when prospects click on a search engine. You have some control over this process because you choose the words that appear on your website.

Of course, most business owners don't wait for clients to find them. When you're trying to reach prospective clients who don't know you exist, you won't meet them for the first time via an advertisement on television.

To get "found" by clients who don't know you, you might write a guest post or appear as a podcast guest. You might get featured in local or national media. You post to social media and (with the right strategy) get past the clutter so your target clients notice you.

When prospects find you, they won't listen to a clever commercial. In fact, they'll most likely be annoyed if you present one. They will be looking for answers to specific questions. Often they're seeking solutions to a problem. They will find those answers in your content and your stories.

When you promote your services online, being sticky brings you more sales than being memorable.

Your audience gets exposed to dozens - maybe hundreds - of offers. Rather than create an emotional association, your goal will be to invite them into your community. You want permission to remain in contact. There's no guarantee they'll ever return to your website or landing page ever again.

That means you offer a lead magnet as a reason to sign up for your emails. You can't send them emails (legally) unless they give you this permission.

You might create the "I've seen you everywhere" with strategic choices: getting booked on podcasts, creating a presence on social media, publishing on popular blogs. But you can't count on repeated exposures the way a television advertiser would.

(2) Your brand plays a different role in your marketing compared to the big companies.

Most of the time, customers know what to expect when they order a beer or buy a t-shirt.

Many small businesses - especially solopreneurs - offer unique services that weren't available even ten years ago. You have a unique challenge to explain what you do and who you are.

When you're a solopreneur, your clients don't know what to expect, even when you name your service, such as "accountant," "massage therapist," or "home stager."

You differentiate your services by the way you deliver them. That goes beyond a slogan or color scheme.

"Build a strong brand" is the answer when...

- you get a lot of queries from prospects who aren't in your target market;
- you have trouble communicating what you do at a networking event;
- clients are surprised at how much (or how little) you charge
- you're not getting referrals because nobody understands what you do or who you serve

- you struggle to find stories to support your strategy (and maybe wonder if you need this whole story thing after all)

(3) Big brands create emotions from imaginary personalities.

There's nothing inherently emotional about a mixture of barley, water, hops, and yeast. Beer doesn't taste like a party or a family gathering, any more than soft drinks taste like sentimental scenes in the ads.

Cola? Sugar, more chemicals, and water.

Sportswear? Just cloth arranged by a designer.

Cat food? Demanding, finicky felines who torture their well-meaning owners.

That's why a lot of consumer products create personalities for their brands.

In fact, when I was teaching Marketing 101, we used to ask questions like, "Imagine this brand were a person. What would you say if you met at a party? Would you want to meet this brand for coffee?"

Your brand reflects your real–not created–personality.

You might relate to your prospects and clients as a good friend - someone you like to hang out with. Or you might be the authoritative expert who's teaching, preaching, and guiding.

You might share a lot of information about your personal life, including your doubts and fears. Or you might remain backstage, encouraging your audience to focus on your services.

You might be warm and caring with lots of big virtual hugs. Or you might be strictly business.

You can decide to build an online personality.

Some people do manage to create a public persona that's distinctly different from their real self. Some invent loving parents, children, and spouses. Sometimes they're very effective: they fit the image their clients want.

But wherever you are, you don't start with a bunch of chemicals and decide they remind you of cute little puppies.

Apart from personality, you have a style of delivering a service. Your style gets based on your personality to some extent, but also by your training, experience, and values.

You start with who you are and frame a message. But...

Chapter 3: Your brand will be bigger than your personal quirks.

When you're a solo service-based business owner, your business brand and personal brand overlap.

You are selling yourself. You're a person with a style of service delivery and marketing.

You might be ...

...a "kid next door" role model for your clients: someone who's promising, "I'm just like you. If I can do this, you can too."

...a "professor" educator who promises clients, "I've got the knowledge and I'll give you some aha moments that will change the way you approach your problem."

...a "passion-driven professional" who advocates for your clients, promising to go the extra mile - always! - "no matter what it takes."

...an "innovator" who offers something no one else does, because of who you are or what you've experienced

...a "celebrity" who's got a following of avid fans and a larger-than-life personality (even if you haven't been on Oprah)

But you're still a business. You're not a good old friend...even if you appear to be.

Your image affects your sales. You need to come across as strong and capable. So while you can't brand like the big guys, you can't brand on personality.

You deliver a strong message...and it's not your mess.

For example, Curt's business involved creating videos for medium-sized companies -mostly training videos, but some demonstration and sales videos too.

From the beginning, Curt realized his clients were hiring him as a person. They weren't dealing with a faceless entity or a big brand. He knew he couldn't brand like a beer company.

When Curt called me about refining his branding strategy, he had gotten lots of advice to "promote yourself as a person."

One marketing coach after another gave him advice like: "People hire you because they like you." "Your clients want to see you as a human." "They want to hear about your flaws and mistakes."

Curt also got a lot of advice about branding on personal quirks:

A marketing specialist suggested that he be brand as "the bald videographer." His head would be shiny.

Another suggested "the renegade videographer."

Still another suggested picking up on Curt's vision with the ironical, "the near-sighted videographer." Well, he did wear glasses with distinctive frames.

Fortunately Curt has a built-in radar for cringeworthy marketing. Even more, he trusts his intuition. He rejected all these solutions before the marketers could send him a bill.

Curt's experience is not unique. Business coaches try to get creative with small businesses.

Branding With Adjectives

Some business owners figure they'll come across as personal by branding with adjectives. They look for good qualities they can share. Two common examples are branding as a maverick and branding as a badass.

Branding as a Maverick

Denise had always identified as a rule-breaker. "I color outside the lines," she says.

When she opened for business as a marketing consultant, she called herself the Maverick Branding Consultant. She joined a crowd of business owners who call themselves rebels, renegades, and yes, mavericks.

The word "renegade" has been embraced by successful companies, such as This Renegade Love[8] (which seems to celebrate people doing things well) and the Jeep Renegade.[9]

Copywriter Dan Kennedy used to describe himself as "The Renegade Millionaire." In the original sales letter, he wrote, "Who else wants to defy all normal, common, ordinary, customary boundaries on making money -- on the speed, the ease, and the independence?"

Does that really sound radical to a business owner? I suspect Dan Kennedy's massive success came in spite of his branding. Of course, when he started, fewer business owners branded on personal quirks. Even fewer were self-identified as Renegades.

The real definition of renegade isn't so positive. Merriam-Webster's online dictionary defines renegade as "a deserter from one faith, cause, or allegiance to another… an individual who rejects lawful or conventional behavior."

However, for many, the term maverick evokes images of the wild and wooly west. Lots of people claim maverick status even if they've thrived in the corporate world, served with

distinction in the military, or fit into a suburban setting with ease.

Branding as a "badass"

The word "badass" has gained popularity as yet another broad-based adjective. Branding yourself as "badass" might suggest you're cool...but you're not unique.

A quick review of books on Amazon reveals dozens with the word "badass" in the title. Jen Sincero created a whole brand around being a badass - books, an organizer, a calendar, and probably more.

At the other extreme, we have Spirituality for Badasses[10] by J. Stewart Dixon, described as "funny" and "irreverent."

Being badass comes with a risk: you're saying to the world, "I'm willing to be different and I'm not afraid of four-letter words."

Imagine meeting someone at a party: "Hi, I'm Jennifer. I'm a badass web designer." Or, "Hi, I'm Manuel. I'm a badass dude."

Whenever I hear people describing themselves as "badass" I wonder if they're forty years old and still trying to be the cool kid on the block.

What's Wrong With Adjective Branding: It's About You

While I've seen many people branded as mavericks or badasses (and sometimes both), I've also run across many more business owners who took the advice to "get personal" to heart.

Let's go back to my experiences. Remember the branding coach who urged me to connect with coffee?

"Since you have high energy," she said, "why don't you brand it with coffee?"

The idea appealed to me. I tried renaming some of my offers. My power hour became the Espresso. My multi-session coaching was the Coffee Pot.

My coach never asked me to connect the dots: Why would clients want to hire a high-energy copywriter? Would this brand appeal to clients who didn't drink coffee? Was coffee-generated energy a positive quality?

I soon gave up on the idea...and the branding consultant.

That's the big problem behind branding on a personal quality.

First, your clients won't always connect the dots...at least the way you want them to.

Second, you have to be careful when you brand yourself as an "expert" or as something special. You can come across as bragging. Any time you use adjectives to describe yourself, you risk losing credibility.

The myth of finding your own voice

Since you have a unique personality, you have your own voice — right? And people know you by your voice.

Many business owners believe it's important to speak in their own voice when they create content – whether they're building a website, writing a sales letter, or developing a course.

When they hire a copywriter, their first question is, "Can you make the copy sound like me?"

As a new copywriter, I embraced this idea. I encouraged clients to record themselves speaking on the phone. I listened to experts who advised, "Write the way you speak."

Now I question the whole concept of "your own voice."

My first clue came when I was writing copy for one of my favorite clients. She'd invited me to write a sales letter for her new program.

"Can you include these two paragraphs from my last sales letter?" she asked. "I really like the way they're written."

So I did. And I showed her the finished page.

You probably see where this is going. She loved everything….except those two paragraphs. "I'd never use those words," she said firmly.

So I took out the paragraphs and replaced them with my own writing.

"Perfect," she said. "Sounds just like me."

And that's when I learned that most people don't know how they sound on paper.

As time went on, I realized prospects were responding to the marketer's message. They didn't really notice the words. They looked for consistency in content.

When I first started with copywriting, I got the advice to "Find your voice." I was encouraged to help my clients find *their* voices. I even wrote a few articles on how to find your voice. Hopefully, they've all been deleted by now.

Because "Find your voice" is really lousy advice, right up there with, "Be vulnerable."

As Tom Kuegler wrote in an article on Medium[11]: *"You don't read your favorite writer because they're a master wordsmith. You read your favorite writer because their ideas are mind-blowing."*

When you're enthused about the content, you barely notice the words.

You may have seen those experiments where people are asked to recognize their own brand of beer or cola. Usually, they can't tell one from another, without labels.

The best copywriters are invisible.

That's right – it's their superpower. They focus on you, the reader.

Think of the way movies and plays draw you into the story. When you start admiring the cleverness of an actor's line, or wondering how they handled a special effect, you've stepped back from the fourth wall. You're no longer caught up in the story.

People who read your content aren't thinking about you.

They're thinking about themselves. They want to solve their problems. When your brand forces your audience to focus on you, you've broken the fourth wall. You're distracting them.

You're not "John the masterful money coach." You're "John the guy who just went through a bad divorce."

So we've seen that a small business can't brand like the "big guys." But they have to resist the temptation to go small, focusing on individual personality quirks. So what do they do?

Chapter 4:
Middle Bear Branding

When you're a small business, "standing out" feels like a delicate balancing act.

Brand like everyone in your industry and you risk becoming invisible. Your company is like one of those houses in a development... the ones celebrated by Pete Seeger when he wrote a song about houses[12] that all look "ticky-tacky" and look just the same.

Some business owners go to the other extreme, especially if they offer a service like coaching or consulting. They make up a name to describe what they offer, such as "Confident Charisma."

The truth is, people want to know what they're buying.

When you're ready to revise your will, you'll look for a lawyer with expertise in estate planning, not a "legacy maximizer coach." When you want to sell your house, you look for a real estate agent or broker, not a "home finder specialist."

If you create a new category, you need a story to go along with it...and you have to get people to listen to the story instead of shrugging away.

It's sort of like Goldilocks and the home she invaded. The three bears were not amused.

Too much innovation? You've lost them. On the Internet, you have just a few seconds to grab attention. You're constantly reminded that, "A confused mind always says no."

Too little? You're viewed as a cookie-cutter solution or as someone who's still stuck in an early business model.

You can think of the result as Middle Bear Branding. It's a two-step process:

First, put yourself in your clients' world. Describing your service in familiar language from their perspective.

Then bring them into your world with a story that (a) responds to their backstory and (b) reinforces your brand

So the "confident charisma" coach becomes "a leadership coach helping clients act and feel confident in new 'over their head' environments." Let's call her Linda.

She tells a story about helping Matthew, a newly-promoted corporate executive. He was just beginning to realize he had been assigned a role that was far more challenging than he'd been led to expect.

The downside was huge, the upside unlikely. He had to appear confident...and Linda's proprietary system gave him the tools to conquer the odds.

The title and description will resonate in Linda's market. The story contains the element of creativity, uniqueness and surprise.

The truth is, we are hard-wired to categorize.

An HBR article[13] summed it up:

"Your mind is a categorization machine, busy all the time taking in voluminous amounts of messy data and then simplifying and structuring it so that you can make sense of the world."

The article emphasizes that categorization can be dangerous and counterproductive. - but it's essential to connecting with clients..

When potential clients hear about your service, they want to put you into a familiar category.

When they hear your name for the first time, they don't have a place to assign your company. You might be easily forgotten. Or you might be assigned to a category that doesn't fit the services you provide.

That's why it's rarely a good idea to come up with creative names to describe what you do. When you describe yourself as a Life Energizer, Creative Catalyst, or Profit Maximizer Coach, you're not helping prospective clients find the mental bucket to assign you.

At a networking event, you might get a polite, "What's that?" On a website, you'll get clickaways. Confusion rarely is a good way to begin a relationship.

That's why I don't support the popular idea of describing your business by function, as in, "I help clients relieve stress."

Do you offer massage, aromatherapy, meditation, EFT tapping, counseling, life coaching or a new technique nobody else is using? Some people will be interested if you offer aromatherapy; others won't, even if they're equally stressed.

Your offer fits a script in the consumer's mind.

You'll be easier to categorize when prospective clients say, "I know someone who did that."

For instance, corporate executives are now hiring publicists and agents for themselves. rather than wait for companies to assign them. They want to take control of their own careers and media presence. If you're a publicist looking to pitch an executive, your success will be easier if your prospective client can say, "I know someone who did that."

On the other hand, when your offer seems irrelevant, it won't become a topic of conversation. I learned this lesson myself when I published my first website[14] on the topic of relocation. My audience resisted.

Big discovery: People will hire planners for parties and weddings. No problem. But hire a coach for a relocation that costs many thousands of dollars more? A move that can turn your life upside down for a long, long time? No way.

Logical? No! Most of us can survive a bad party. But if you move to a destination that's wrong for you, you're looking at *years* of misery and thousands of dollars in moving back, therapy, and maybe even losing your job if you don't fit in.

The reality is, there aren't that many relocation coaches. A lack of competition almost always means, "Nobody cares."

More important, it doesn't generate conversations like, "My relocation coach is better than anybody else's." The most important way to generate buzz is to get your audience to talk about their experience with you.

What could I do?

I soon decided to position myself as a career coach. I noted that I had expertise in relocation. The concept of "career coach" was familiar to most of my potential clients. Usually when they were seeking relocation coaching (and could afford to pay the going rate), they were simultaneously making a career move.

When I tried to position as a "relocation coach," I simply baffled my audience. They had no category and no script. When I was "just another career coach," my services got lost in a maze of look-alike coaches, all promoting similar services.

My Middle Bear position, as a career consultant with a specialty of relocation, worked well for me. Some clients weren't interested in relocation. At the time, though, any career change required considering the option to relocate. A lot of my clients found their dream job was located in a place they couldn't bear to live.

The Secret to Middle Bear Branding: Find their backstory

In his book Tell To Win[16], Peter Guber demonstrates the impact of a customer's backstory. A producer needed to get Alice Walker's approval to produce her book, *The Color Purple*, as a stage play. Alice was the customer; the producer was, in a real sense, doing the selling.

Guber coached the producer to expect resistance. Alice had gotten a negative backlash from the black community after her book was produced as a movie. The producer needed to address Alice's backstory -- not directly, but with a new story.

Jack Dorsey, Founder of Twitter and Square, says their company spends a lot of time writing "user narratives." These narratives read like a play: "They go to a coffee shop in downtown Chicago..."

Everyone can relate to the story at all levels from designers to those in "the business side of the house," says Dorsey.

Business owners rarely have access to individual backstories when developing copy for websites and sales letters. But often you can identify common backstories, even without an intensive, high-priced research effort. And as you work with more clients, you'll start to see a common theme among backstories, although the details may differ.

For instance, a business owner named Christina Hills[17] runs programs targeting prospects with backstories related to building websites. Those backstories have a common theme: high expectations followed by disappointing results. They go something like this:

"I've spent thousands of dollars on web design and have nothing to show for it but a ton of credit card debt."

"The website looks beautiful but if I need to change one word, it's going to cost me $65. Minimum."

"My web developer disappeared, taking my passwords with him."

And for my relocation service, I positioned my offer to fall under the umbrella of career change -- a topic I care about even more.

"Did you know IBM stands for "I've been moved?"

"We just moved here. My wife got an offer she couldn't refuse."

"My company just moved me here and I hate it."

"Should I accept that offer? I don't know if I can live there."

Those were some of the backstories that helped me target my book, Making the Big Move[15].

Your Customer's Back Story Helps You Generate Buzz

When offering a new service, it's often difficult for your prospects to relate your offer to their pain point. They may not even be aware they have a pain point. But what's on their mind? What will they vent about? You got it...their story.

Section 2: Small Business Branding Begins With Your Story Archetype

After working with hundreds of clients and studying even more, I've identified five marketing styles (you could also call them personas) that successful solopreneurs apply to their brand: the five archetypes.

When I analyze the marketing materials of other small businesses, invariably each business has adopted one of these five archetypes. I've yet to find a small, service-based business that doesn't fit this framework.

Most businesses are completely unaware - after all, they haven't even heard of me or the five archetypes. Yet they choose stories, writing styles, and approaches that consistently fall into the pattern of one archetype.

The archetype serves as a container for their brand. The rest of their marketing feels like water flowing downhill.

Why does it work?

Your reputation as an expert is built on the credibility you generate.

Credibility in turn is based on consistency. When you show up the same way, over and over, you build trust.

When business owners think of consistency, they often think of sending out an email the same day every week. They think of choosing colors and type fonts so they'll appear consistently in print.

But you can also be consistent with the stories you tell and the words you use.

Do you talk about "crushing the competition" and "exploding with possibility?" Or do you talk about "supporting your clients" and "insightful decision-making?" Are you warm and caring or combative and aggressive?

Your archetype gives you a framework to present ideas consistently without being repetitive. Your archetype helps you choose stories and words that represent you consistently. When you see a list of "power words," you know which ones make the most sense for you.

Each archetype is defined by a promise.

For instance, I'm an Educator archetype. My promise is, "I have information that will help you succeed. When you learn from me, and when you apply this knowledge, you'll be successful."

All my communication is directed to sharing knowledge, simplifying processes, and giving my audience a new angle on marketing. I tell stories to make a point or explain a complex idea. I tell stories about "Why these stories succeed and those don't." I make the point, "This isn't rocket science."

When I'm tempted to follow the advice to "let people get to know you as a person," I drive away prospects. They aren't interested in my cats, my workouts in the gym, or my fanatical dedication to reading murder mysteries.

In contrast…

Role Models promise, "I'm just like you. If I can do this, you can too." Role Models share stories about "How I Got From There To Here." A variation is, "How My Client Followed Me From There To Here."

They tell stories like, "Writing was really hard for me till I found a system that worked." But they also tell personal stories to show they're human: "How I planted my new garden" or "How we chose a new car." They talk about their families, too.

Innovators promise, "I hold the key to solving a big problem. You've been searching a long time, and I'm the only one who can offer it."

Their promise seems unbelievable to their prospects. They seem to promise a pot of gold at the end of the rainbow.

However, there's a catch. New ideas scare people. So to gain credibility and overcome fear, Innovators tell stories about how their innovation helped others get a big win.

Innovators brand with stories like, "My client Timothy spent $5000 on his first website and got zero clients. With my system, he built his own for $50 and clients have to join a waiting list to see him."

Passionate Advocates promise, "I'll go the extra mile for you."

They tell stories that begin, "My client called me at 3 AM when he got in a jam." They share stories of how they rode in like the cavalry and saved the day.

Celebrities probably aren't reading this book. They're not real celebrities: they just market like people in People magazine.

Their promise is, "I'm qualified to advise you because I've reached this level of success." They tell stories that reinforce their identity as "so successful they do whatever they want and break all the rules."

Their stories read like stories in the popular press. Clients buy into the belief, "If they're successful–or such outrageous rule breakers–they must be good." And they often are.

This section offers you a closer look at all 5 archetypes. Later we'll talk about why it's important to understand all five, not just your own. In the Resources section at the end of this book, I offer you access to a free quiz to test your own archetype.

Chapter 5:
The Role Model

Cindy Bidar is a successful business coach, working mostly with solopreneurs. She sends an email to her mailing list almost every day. Each email begins with a short anecdote. She usually takes these stories from her personal life or her early days in business..

Cindy likes to tell a story about starting her own business:

"My husband asked, 'How will you know how to do all these things to help people?'"

"I replied, 'If other people know how to use this software, I can too. I can use the search engines. I can take classes. And each time I learn something,I can teach it to someone else.'"

That's a Role Model. They make the promise, "I'm just like you. If I can do it, you can too."

Role Models are the kids who were a year ahead of you in high school. They gave you insider tips that weren't in the handbook. They showed you how to stay out of trouble–because they'd been there themselves.

They're the neighbor who shows you around when you move into the neighborhood. They're the colleague who shares the inside information of "how things really get done around here."

They don't claim to be superior. They assure you, "I once was where you are. You'll be here someday."

Role Models thrive on hard work. When I talk to Role Models, I remember the late Pat Summitt who coached women's basketball teams at Tennessee. She would say, "We will win because we will out-work you.

Like basketball players, Role Models tend to be competitive - in a friendly way - and they like to win. They're the team leaders who bring out the capabilities in their clients and the people they hire.

Therefore, Role Models enter business contests enthusiastically. They aren't afraid to aim for the championship and to do the work, systematically, to get there. They're the ones who remain on the basketball court, practicing their 3-point shots, long after the rest of the squad has gone home.

Role Models honestly believe they're not exceptional people and they definitely don't believe in luck. They come across as genuinely humble. Sometimes they claimed to be amazed at their own success.

The Role Model's Superpower: They have "court sense."

Like top basketball players, they're aware of what's going on with their market. Like basketball players who see an opening and get to the basket, Role Models instinctively identify gaps in their marketplace and quickly create products to fill them.

How Role Models Relate To Their Clients

Role Models make the claim, "Here's what I did and I can teach you how to do the same thing."

The Role Model relates to her clients on a highly personal level and she markets herself as smart, straightforward and approachable. Success depends on being ; you'll feel you know her even more than you do.

One Role Model got calls from her ezine subscribers, total strangers who called to say, "Hi, we're in town – can we have lunch?"

Another Role Model Story

Marketing coach Connie Ragen Green shares her origin story frequently. She pivoted from working as an elementary school teacher and real estate agent to running a successful online empire.

In one story, Connie ran into a couple she hadn't seen for a long time. She invited them to come visit her. They said, "We can't. We're retired. We don't have money for travel and we can't do anything."

Connie told them how she's been making money with online marketing.

"Do you think we could do that?" they asked nervously.

"Of course!" Connie said, following up with some suggestions and links to resources.

Several months later, Connie saw them again and repeated the invitation. They said, "Oh no, we can't. We're too busy. We followed your suggestions and started working on the Internet. We've got another vacation planned for next week."

This story is perfect for Connie's audience: people who don't have much experience online. Many of them are scared. This story delivers one of Connie's core values: "Anyone can do this if they are willing to learn."

If you're looking for some good examples of "If I can do it, you can do it," check out some of Connie Ragen Green's story-filled books.

My favorite is her story of a road trip. In her first days, she experienced severe leg pain. She could barely walk. Ignoring the advice of well-meaning doctors, she continued her journey. She doesn't minimize the pain. She just models a way of responding.

Jon Morrow uses his background also. Jon became a quadriplegic following a horrible auto accident. Deciding he didn't want to depend on the stingy survival offerings of the US government, he became an Internet guru and blogging expert. Today he earns enough to hire his own staff to care for him and treat him the way he wants to be treated.

Jon doesn't say, "If I can do it, you can." But he does show that he learned from his experiences. One of my favorite examples is Jon's story of why he's become such a successful persuader. "I can't do anything for myself. I have to persuade people to do things for me."

Yet another example comes from a personal fitness trainer I'll call Bob. When I knew Bob, he promoted his business with images of himself in his earlier incarnation: very overweight and unfit. Bob found himself with all the signs of a heart attack waiting to happen (as he likes to say): high blood pressure, high cholesterol, pre-diabetic, and more.

For his own health, Bob began exercising and eating mindfully. He developed a program for himself, then became certified as a professional trainer. He attracts clients who relate to his struggles and want to look the way he looks now.

Content Creation For Role Models

Role models present most of their content in the form of first-person stories. They tend to be prolific course creators. They favor a down-to-earth strategy for courses - lots of step-by-step.

Role Models send emails to their mailing list frequently - sometimes every day, as Cindy Bidar does. Their emails serve two functions. They deepen relationships and they sell.

When you're getting emails that open with a story and at least one call to action, you're most likely dealing with a Role Model..

One Role Model marketer told me directly, "I start with a story from my own experience. Maybe I took a walk in the woods this morning. Then I relate that story to something I want to share with my clients."

This method might work for Celebrities, who often share stories of personal experiences associated with exotic locales and "living the dream" opportunities. But Celebrities assume, rightly, that their audiences crave information about them.

Educators, Innovators, and Passionate Advocates will use personal stories only to support a point they want to make. They don't set out to tell a story because it's personal, because they don't connect with clients by "getting to know you."

Where Role Models Go Wrong

The Role Model thrives on saying, "I'm just like you."

But she also needs to command respect. She talks about how hard she worked and how many problems she's overcome. But she can't afford to be viewed as a victim.

Role Models often treasure a story that has special meaning for them -- a perfect story to share with a colleague or a live event.

But that story may not be the most effective for their marketing.

The RIGHT way to do this is to say something like:

"When I started I didn't know anything about marketing with funnels. So I hired a business coach and read everything I could get my hands on. I created a technique that I teach to people who could barely turn on their computer when they started."

The WRONG way is to say,

"I was only a B student in college. My family wasn't rich. I hustled my way into an acting job in my twenties. When I started my business, I only knew how to reach people and understand what motivated them.

"And here I am, with perfectly highlighted hair (not a trace of frizz) and a killer smile of white straight teeth (not everyone can get this no matter what your dentist says), rocking a pair of jeans and a t-shirt like a supermodel. If I can do it, you can do it."

All I can say is, "You must be kidding."

First of all, as a former college professor, I can tell you that lots of people who went on to get PhDs and teach weren't straight-A students. One of my most successful colleagues couldn't spell. He had to get an assistant to review his many well-published papers.

Being a B student who's "from an ordinary family" hardly places you at a disadvantage. Companies often preferred to hire B-minus students.

If you were a cheerleader, sorority girl, or model, kudos to you! Martha Stewart worked as a model to earn money in college.

But either you were incredibly lucky (someone saw you at a coffee shop and invited you to be on the cover of Vogue) or you knew how to work a system and tailor your looks and style to reach your goal. You understood how to appeal to tough-minded judges.

Growing up poor doesn't help your brand either. The vast majority of your audience won't have experience with the welfare system, unless you've chosen to work with a non-profit that specializes in helping people pull themselves up by their own bootstraps.

By the time you're earning enough to brag about your private air travel, $400 haircut and bi-level condo in Manhattan, your family history will no longer define you. What got you here won't take you there.

Role models need to focus on turning outward. If you're a Role Model, focus on what inspires you, what you learned, and most important–why your clients will benefit from learning about your experience.

Will you gain more credibility? Will they find it easier to approach you? Will they be more confident about taking the next steps or putting themselves in your hands?

Good stories start with strategy, not struggle. You can take it from there.

Chapter 6: The Innovator

When Christina Hills started her first business, she offered courses to help business owners set up a product that represented a major innovation at that time, an all-in-one cart, affiliate program, and email system. This product qualified as the focus of her business. It was complex, with a steep learning curve, but it was the best game in town.

Christina marketed her business as solving a big problem. People needed the cart to collect money. She could teach them how to use the cart to get the best benefit from its many features.

As business owners turned to other shopping carts, Christina changed her business model to focus on website development. Her timing was perfect.

Web-savvy businesses were getting fed up with temperamental web developers who decamped to Tahiti mid-project, leaving them stranded without their passwords. Meanwhile, Wordpress was becoming the industry standard for large and small businesses. Now an ordinary person could put up a quality website without writing even one line of code.

Christina targeted business owners who were, as the saying goes, "mad as hell and determined not to take it anymore." Her message unabashedly attacked the "evil webmasters," resonating with the mood of her audience. One of her early promotional videos satirized Little Red Riding Hood with the webmaster featured as the wolf.

Wordpress can be intimidating to non-tech business owners, but it's not that hard to learn when you've got someone to guide you through the process. For many business owners, Christina would become that guide.

Many individuals and businesses claim to teach Wordpress to businesses. They offer videos and manuals.

Christina's innovation: a new-to-the-world teaching method that would be hard for others to duplicate. Each "student" in her course gets a platform to practice building Wordpress websites. They can play with themes, colors and type fonts, with no risk of discovery from the search engines.

Christina's brand positions her as an Innovator.

The Innovator's Promise and Delivery

The Innovator's promise has two parts:

1. They promise to solve a specific, significant problem that's extremely obvious and painful to their audience.

2. They promise uniqueness: they're the only ones who can solve that problem.

Ideally, the innovator's solution can't be copied easily. The marketplace has created several barriers to entry.

It's important to understand that anyone can be innovative in their business. Not everyone who is innovative is an Innovator.

Creativity leads to credibility. When you know your field well enough to develop an innovation, you've gone beyond the basics. You're not just a cookie-cutter service business.

In particular, many Educators create frameworks that become the foundation of their businesses. In fact, innovation helps entrepreneurs gain credibiity. I've innovated myself, with the archetype framework.

The difference is in the positioning and the promise.

Innovators position themselves as offering something new that can't be found anywhere else. Their whole business is built around their innovation.

Educators position themselves as offering knowledge. They promise to simplify concepts and create "aha" moments of awareness that lead to business breakthroughs.

How Innovators Relate to Their Clients

Innovators make you think of superheroes. They're the ones who fly in out of nowhere and present you with a practical solution to your problem - a problem you feared would never go away.

Innovators don't need to relate personally. Their clients are so happy to get their problems solved. They're less concerned with building a close relationship.

However, we do see exceptions. Sometimes the Innovation comes directly out of the Innovator's experience.

Business Coach Alicia Forest, introduced a new model of successful business — prioritizing free time.

When Alicia started her business, her priority was spending time with her family and children. She wanted summers off. Since the day she started her business, she never looked back.

"I've watched others soar ahead of me," she says, "only to watch them be crushed under the pressure of working too hard, lose their marriages, hardly spend time with their kids, gain a lot of weight and suffer from other major health issues, and be absolutely miserable by the monster they created.

"Meanwhile, I've grown my business, steadily and surely, without one single sacrifice along the way."

Alicia does talk about her family, particularly as her children have grown. Unlike Role Models, she doesn't share personal stories to create a human connection. Unlike Educators, she's not using specific stories as metaphors for concepts. She's using her stories as evidence that her method works.

For instance, she'll say, "My daughter was having a tough time in college. I was able to drive down immediately to be with her. I didn't have to ask permission. And I was able to maintain my revenues."

The Innovator's Superpowers

An innovator's superpower (like their promise) has two parts.

Their first superpower is their intuition, which operates efficiently as a radar detector.

Innovators instinctively know what people are looking for. To be sure, they do research. They might ask questions like, "What's the most popular software that people struggle with?" Yet ultimately, when the research is done, someone has to interpret the data and make a decision. That's where intuition comes in.

The Innovator's success depends on identifying a problem that will be (a) extremely pressing, urgent, and possibly painful; and (b) shared by a large number of prospects who can pay for a solution at premium prices.

These qualities are necessary for an Innovator to succeed...but they're not sufficient.

Successful Innovators also need a second superpower: communicating a novel solution to a skeptical audience. They take credibility to a whole new level.

Many Innovator clients have spent long hours - even days and months - seeking an answer. They may have encountered false promises and misleading marketers. An Innovator knows how to build trust.

Innovators with integrity don't come up with a series of promises. They use marketing to show they understand where the audience is coming from.

Christina Hills knew that the term "evil webmasters" would not be too strong for her audience. Anyone who's been through a frustrating website makeover will have some pretty strong emotions around their tech support.

The most successful Innovators go one step further: they create a phrase or expression that's accurate, descriptive, and memorable.

Christina Hills named her program the Website Creation Workshop - short, memorable, and descriptive.

Alicia Forest talks about generating a full-time income with part-time hours. That's easy for her clients to understand.

The Innovator's Challenge: "Can you believe this?!"

Researchers have long known that customers resist innovation[18]. In the world of products, few innovations reach commercial success.

Innovation requires you to change the way you think about solving a problem. It's easy to recognize resistance in the world of products. If you're used to baking and broiling, a microwave will seem challenging. If you're used to getting cash from a human teller, ATMs will seem annoying and intimidating.

Today's clients and customers still resist innovation for the same reasons. If you're used to turning your website over to a developer, the notion of DIY may seem daunting. You have to believe you can DIY even if you're not a tech specialist.

When you're marketing in the online space, you have an additional challenge. Most of your prospective clients will have been burned by other people's promises, sometimes more than once. You have to get past their disbelief. And that barrier can be huge.

Therefore, while role Models need to be relatable and Educators need to be clear, innovators need to be credible. When an Innovator presents a new offer, the market reacts with, "This sounds too good to be true."

Some innovations require an additional layer of trust. If you're got a new way to handle payment systems or provide a new remedy for a health problem, you'll likely meet more resistance, because you're playing a high-stakes game. Health and money are hot button topics.

Stories Innovators Tell

Innovator stories meet the credibility challenge head-on. Their stories convey the message, "See - this thing really works!"

Innovators tell stories of clients who succeeded with their innovations. Their websites feature heart-felt stories of clients who succeeded beyond their wildest dreams.

Innovator stories follow a predictable pattern:

I had a terrible problem. Here's how it affected me. I discovered this solution. Here's how it made a difference.

For example, Christina Hills created a new method of learning Wordpress, combining design and marketing. An effective story might follow this structure:

"I'm a solopreneur in a service-based business. I hired a web developer for $5000. I was left with a so-so website. Worst of all, I couldn't make changes without breaking the design. I'd have to spend $150 to hire tech support each time I wanted to change a date or change a paragraph on the home page.

"After taking Christina's course, I created a beautiful website. I can make changes myself, easily. I'm getting more leads and more clients, too."

Another Innovator, a system developer, created an app to match people who needed event space with groups that had space to rent. He could tell a story like this:

"We needed a space for a child's birthday party. We didn't want to rent a hotel ballroom. We wanted to bring our own food. After asking around, we heard about a church that would rent out its assembly room and kitchen for a small fee.

"We realized many other people would have the same need. So we created an app to match event planners with available spaces."

Marketing Strategies

Unlike Role Models, Educators and some Celebrities, you'll rarely see Innovators with podcasts. Their focus is on solving a specific problem, once and for all.

They're constantly needing an influx of clients, not a series of clients returning over and over . Once a client has grasped their solution, there's no need to return. They're usually not offering a funnel of products; they're offering solutions.

Innovators find creative ways to attract traffic and get new clients.

Christina bases her marketing on affiliate programs. She pays generous commissions, inspiring many other business owners to promote her product for a sales commission. This strategy gets Christina in front of thousands of prospective clients who fit her target, with no advertising.

In contrast, Alicia downplays her limited affiliate program. She uses social media to invite prospective clients to free, short online courses and programs. She also offers business coaching on an ongoing basis, so she takes advantage of repeat purchases from clients who appreciate her innovation.

Innovators use email marketing to announce special programs and training opportunities. They rarely begin with an anecdote or story about themselves. They don't use the "nurturing" emails associated with Role Models.

Innovators may offer one-to-one consulting, but their big focus almost always involves enrolling clients into classes and programs.

Innovators might offer additional opportunities for clients who experienced success. Christina offers short courses on using graphics and other tools to enhance websites. But they don't create opportunities to "stay on my list because you might need me someday."

Should you brand as an Innovator?

Branding as an Innovator requires consistent attention to the problem being solved. You won't be sharing stories about yourself. Your focus will be on helping your followers implement the solution, through training or software or both.

If that's appealing, consider branding as an innovator. But you could also consider becoming an Educator. That's a very popular choice for consultancy businesses, as we'll soon see.

Chapter 7: The Educator

Jacquette Timmons describes herself as a financial behaviorist. She offers behavioral-based financial coaching and training to professionals, including lawyers with top-tier firms and senior corporate executives. Her copy refers to challenges associated with donations and investments, a sign she's dealing with high-end clients.

While Jacquette has developed a unique approach to financial coaching, she doesn't position herself as an Innovator. She uses multiple modalities to communicate with her audience - blog posts, website pages, a podcast, and a book. She presents ideas that encourage her readers to think more deeply and creatively.

Jacquette sends a long email every Sunday night, a thousand words or more. She sends long, thoughtful messages that aren't necessarily "How to do X." They're never listicles.

Some of her titles have been, "The Cultural Tendency to Want Money to Be Easy" "Do You See How Today's Traditions Build Tomorrow's " and "This is How You Know You're Suffering from Financial Trauma."

Jacquette creates "aha" moments from the very first page of her website: "You Don't Manage Money, You Manage Choices."

When we analyze Jacquette's marketing, we can see that her content consistently reinforces her brand. She consistently fits the model of the Educator Archetype.

Promise and Deliver:

The Educator might be a business consultant, a specialized tax lawyer, a fashion consultant or a financial advisor...or just about any type of professional service-based business. She's often hired after prospects come across her books, videos, or webinars.

The Educator promises, "I have a lot of knowledge about your problem. When you buy my products and services, you're buying into my promise: 'If you apply the knowledge I share, you will reach success."

The best Educators deliver "aha" moments. Their clients frequently say, "He gave me a new perspective," or, "I have a totally new way to approach this activity."

But the Educator doesn't try to impress clients with esoteric language and a large vocabulary. They wear their knowledge lightly.

How Educators Relate To Their Clients

Educators relate to their clients as teachers relate to adult students. However, they're not high up on a pedestal. They're colleagues and friends. You'll rarely find Educators talking down to their clients. They're respectful.

Many Educators maintain mailing lists and collect subscribers. Yet it's rare to find Educators who write to their lists every day. Several write long, thoughtful weekly emails that can become blog posts or even books.

The Educator's Superpowers

Educators have two superpowers.

FIrst, they get the big picture.

When they're explaining why an email marketing system works, they'll be aware of the current economic environment. They'll understand the reasons why email marketing has become critical. They may study the psychology behind subscribers' motivation. They may rely on their own experience to provide additional depth.

When they're helping a client develop a video presentation, they'll know why video serves as the most effective vehicle for the client's specific purpose. They'll understand the message and brand functions that drive the script. They'll know how to use tech and design to make it all come together.

They may even understand how to motivate reluctant executives to get in front of the camera - and look like they know what they're doing.

Second, they know how to make this knowledge seem easy.

They're the ones who easily transform a vague, complex process into a step-by-step program. They take something that looks complicated and say, "This isn't rocket science."

And they usually make it fun.

A Role Model client will say, "I didn't think I could do it, but you gave me the confidence because I related to you."

An Educator's client will say, "I didn't think I could understand what I need to do, but you've made it seem simple."

When your clients frequently say, "This seemed so complicated and you made it easy," you're probably marketing with the Educator archetype.

You might also hear, "I've never heard anyone explain it that way before."

Stories Educators Tell

Educators like to tell concept stories.

You can learn more about "concept stories" in my earlier book, *Grow Your Business One Story at a Time*.

Briefly, a concept story explains a complex or novel idea, often teaching a lesson. And the best concept stories also create an "aha" moment

A classic example of a concept story is the "drunk and the car keys." It goes something like this:

A man stumbles around a lamppost in the middle of a parking lot. A police officer comes by and asks him, "What are you doing?" '

"I'm looking for my car keys," the man says.

The officer starts to help. "Did you lose them over here?" he asks.

"No! I dropped them over there in the alley."

"So why are you looking here?"

"Because it's dark over there."

This story explains a concept: Too many of us waste time doing something ineffective because it's easy, but we don't solve the real problem.

Once you understand the point of a concept story, you'll see examples everywhere.

For example, in my earlier book I wrote about a woman who wanted to be an internationally recognized keynote speaker. She invested time in Toastmasters--a worthwhile club, but one that provides few pathways to achieve her dream.

"I don't have any other way to get there," she said.

The keys were over there; she was looking over here, in the light.

Using a Concept Story To Illustrate a Marketing Concept

The Marketing Funnel

Ian Brodie tells a story that explains the concept of the marketing funnel. Briefly, it goes like this:

James, a young handyman, knocks on his door, offering to clean the gutters for £20 (about $35). Ian and his family didn't know James, but they did need the job done and they didn't feel like climbing up to DIY. For just $35, they figured, why not? As they were paying James, he offered to do some deck maintenance, also for a reasonable price. He worked extremely hard and got the job done well.

As he left, James said casually, "You know, if you've got any other jobs you need doing – painting, repairs, anything, just give me a call". James ended up painting the hallways.

As Ian summarizes, "From what started out as a small job to clean out our gutters, James ended up with a tidy 4 figure sum."

From this story, most business owners will readily understand the concept of a marketing funnel...even though many marketing consultants manage to make the idea seem complex, mysterious and worthy of a four-figure training investment.

The Business Mindset

For another example, Tara McMullin illustrates the concept of a business mindset - something that's not always clear to business owners, even those with years of experience.

Tara shares a story[19] about her husband, Sean. One year he decided to get serious about Novel Writing Month, so he changed his whole style of work.

Instead of working at the kitchen table, he went to a coworking space. He scheduled his time to make writing a priority. This shift changed his working style and his outcome. Armed with this new mindset, he completed his novel. The concept? A change in concept leads to a change in behavior.

Educators refer to their personal lives when they want to illustrate a concept.

Role Models want their audiences to know them as three-dimensional people who can be, well, role models. Celebrities know their audiences want to peek behind the curtain. Educators will talk about themselves when it's the best way to make their point.

Tara didn't tell her story as a way to help her audience get to know her better. She had an important point she wanted to make. She found an example close to home, which just happened to be the best story to illustrate her point.

Where Educators Go Wrong

Educators love to teach. They like to talk, write, and share their knowledge. As a result, they often seem to be teaching rather than marketing. It's important for Educators to add Calls to Action and invitations to Buy.

Educators tend to feel more like...well, educators...than marketers. As a copywriter, I often work with Educators who want to communicate knowledge but also inspire their audience to take action. They want to be approachable and friendly but their audience doesn't want them to be as personal as a Role Model.

Some Educators add a tip jar to their websites. They use software that says to visitors, "Like what you're reading? Buy me a coffee!"

I used to think a tip jar would detract from the Educator's image, but I was wrong. The truth is their website visitors and newsletter subscribers gain a great deal of useful information. A "buy me a coffee" button becomes the virtual equivalent of "let's go have coffee and I'll pick your brain."

Of course, like most business owners, Educators learn not to fall for this ploy. Most of us won't share valuable information - sometimes worth thousands of dollars - for a cappuccino. But if enough people buy the cappuccinos without asking for private time, the information sharing becomes profitable. Hence the tip jar.

For Educators, teaching can be more effective than selling.

Their audiences don't need to be sold. They listen to the Educator's story and think, "I want to learn more."

I signed up for one of Tara McMullin's programs when I saw her framework, explaining different ways people carried out their marketing.

"That makes so much sense!" I said. "I wish I'd heard this before."

That's a common response to Educator marketing. For an Educator, an "aha" moment often turns into a sale.

Educators begin with something they want to share with their audiences.

If you're an Educator, you'll be passionate about your business focus. You'll be aware of the hot topics in the field. You'll keep track of what's being spoken and published on key topics.

As you pay attention, you'll realize your audience cares about certain questions. You'll want to help them answer those questions.

Soon you begin to suspect, "Everybody else has got this wrong."

Educators rarely waste time criticizing others who promote cookie-cutter solutions. They prepare their own. They are able to explain - in depth - why their solution will help the members of their audience. They'll package their solutions into marketable brands.

Unlike Innovators, they rarely develop catchy slogans and memorable names. They present their ideas in a straightforward way. They don't directly inspire action: they give their audience food for thought, which can later be transformed into action steps.

Educators also send less frequent emails. They begin with an idea and find a story to match, which may or may not be a personal story. Sometimes a story inspires them to share insights that lead to insights and aha moments. Those stories aren't necessarily personal: they could even be news stories.

For instance, Tara McMullin is a quintessential Educator. She's got a big following as a business thought leader but keeps a fairly low profile (unlike, for instance, Dorie Clark or Tim Ferriss, who are also Educators).

Tara wrote a longish article for Medium, inspired by a Twitter post. An exhausted parent sought advice on dealing with overwhelm.

Tara was horrified by the "positive thinking" advice this parent received. Instead, Tara wrote, "We deserve to have our limitations and circumstances acknowledged. We deserve guidance that recognizes what we deal with and what we've already accomplished."

Throughout the article, Tara focuses on the cruelty of the positive thinkers.

Is she a parent herself? A Role Model absolutely would let us know; a childless Role Model might make reference to her adopted nieces and nephews (possibly leaving out the adoption part and turning them into daughters and sons). She'd say, "I've been there. I know what it's like."

But Tara's got a different promise. Her promise is, "I have a lot of knowledge. When you apply my knowledge, you'll increase your odds of success." She demonstrates her knowledge by sharing insights, demonstrating her analytical skill, and creating aha moments.

Like Innovators, Educators are focused. Unlike Innovators, Educators typically focus on broad-based opportunities that apply to a variety of problems.

Chapter 8: The Passionate Advocate

"I negotiated with the warden to meet with the young man and spent the weekend on the phone, getting witnesses and documents. It turned out the young man was in the US legally and we were able to get him released and returned home to a very happy mom in California."

Immigration attorney Carlos Batara tells this story.

But you don't have to be a serious business to fit this archetype. A wedding planner could share this story:

"The bride wanted lots of flowers for her wedding! We chose stunning arrangements --just what the bride wanted. Her flowers arrived on time but they weren't exactly what we'd asked for -- and they were beginning to wilt!

"We got into our van and drove over an hour to a florist in a neighboring town. We manually put together new arrangements and got them in place just in time for a noon wedding. Everything went off perfectly! And you can see the florals in every photo they added to their gallery."

The Passionate Advocate's Promise

Passionate Advocates base their branding on the promise, "I will go the extra mile for you." Sometimes it's phrased as "whatever it takes."

Relationship to Clients

Passionate Advocates relate to their audiences as a helper to someone in need. Their clients can't solve their own problems no matter how hard they try.

Passionate Advocates work with clients who have gotten themselves into a jam or who face a significant challenge that carries consequences, emotional or financial.

The clients feel powerless. They can't extricate themselves from the problem. They desperately need help.

"This woman was frantic because her son had been picked up by the authorities and disappeared into the system. We tracked him down to a prison in Arizona. I got there on Friday. The hearing was scheduled for Monday and this prison normally did not allow lawyers to see clients on weekends.

Passionate Advocates understand their clients' emotions, especially their fears. When they market their services, communicate that they're easy to work with. They won't be judgmental.

Sometimes they communicate their support very subtly.

For instance, many people want to provide for their pets when they make their wills. They want to be sure their attorney will take these requests seriously.

One trust-and-estates attorney made sure his website includes photos of himself with his two large dogs. I don't know if he did this deliberately, but he's sending a clear message: I totally "get" that pets are members of the family.

Examples of Passionate Advocates

The best way to learn about Passionate Advocates is to look up the website and blog of personal injury, criminal or DUI/DWI lawyers. They're dealing with people who are under extreme stress. Clients find them by referral or by searching online.

Of course, Passionate Advocates who are lawyers face a particularly daunting task. They have to convince the client they're sympathetic without being able to say, "I've been there." Few criminal lawyers, for instance, have criminal records, because few lawyers are allowed to practice if they've been convicted of serious crimes.

This content from the website of a criminal law firm[20] offers a good example of the type of content a Passionate Advocate might write:

Our criminal lawyers understand that the days after an arrest or a call from a detective are both frightening and stressful for you and your family members. Whether you have been charged with a misdemeanor or a felony, you have a lot of questions, and you want to know what is going to happen next. Most importantly, you have critical decisions that need to be made right away."

This firm does a particularly good job of painting word pictures to capture the emotions of a potential client. They demonstrate credibility because they understand exactly what the client needs: answers to a lot of questions and help with decisions.

They also do a great job of communicating how they're non-judgmental. Their potential client needs help. That's all that matters.

Another law firm, this one focused on estate planning, includes a message about their convenient hours and scheduling flexibility: "*Whatever works for you, we will make it happen.*"

Other services that deal with clients at emotionally intense moments could position themselves as Passionate Advocates.

I once met a banker whose company promised 24/7 access to their premium clients. "I've fielded calls at 3 AM," she told me.

A divorce coach[21], Jessica Ashley, seems to position herself as a Passionate Advocate. I've never met Jessica, but her website does a good job of communicating her archetype. She specifically describes her role as a "fierce advocate" and "compassionate listener" for newly divorced moms. She acknowledges that some women feel overwhelmed and even embarrassed with the supportive line, "Your life is bigger than one relationship."

Passionate Advocates tell two kinds of stories.

First, they tell stories about their clients.

"The house had been on the market for months. Prospective buyers came to open houses and showings, but the property gained only a few low-ball offers. After we did just a little bit of staging the house got two offers above the asking price."

Second, they tell stories about why they're so passionate.

"When I was growing up, my family had tenants who were late paying their rent. When they were late we had trouble putting food on the table. Now I'm passionate about helping my clients collect the debts they're lawfully owed."

The Superpower of Passionate Advocates: Knowing the ins and outs of complex systems.

When I visited Egypt I saw a surprising example of a Passionate Advocate. Our tour group had gone on an excursion to a market in Cairo when we realized we'd covered more distance than we planned. We were quite a distance from our hotel, very hot and very tired.

Our tour director pulled out his cell phone and quietly made a call. Within minutes, a white van pulled up, just big enough to take all of us. The tour director obviously knew the driver. After a hair-raising, high-speed drive through back alleys, we were back at the hotel in time for dinner.

Although I was amazed at this performance, I later met someone who'd married an Egyptian and knew the country well.

"People who work in tourism maintain a tight network," she said. "They know each other well. He would know there were vans hanging around certain places, in between jobs. And he'd know all the drivers."

To succeed, Passionate Advocates must be insiders.

Carlos, the immigration lawyer, keeps up with immigration laws and follows cases in all the federal courts. He knows when a new ruling will make it easier - or harder - for his client to succeed.

Wedding planners work closely with vendors. Like the Egyptian tour director, they know who to call when something goes wrong at the eleventh hour.

Home stagers know what appeals to potential buyers right now. They have to stay on top of trends. One year, a certain shade of blue will signal "contemporary." The next year, off-white will be "in." They also know what buyers look for when they're viewing homes; often a small change will drive them away.

Challenges of Passionate Advocates

Passionate Advocates face two challenges. Their greatest challenge comes when setting expectations for their prospects. Unless you're really careful about setting boundaries, you could end up exhausted, unsatisfied, and burned out.

Lawyers lose cases, no matter how competent they are or how hard they work. Laws can change overnight, so a new client can't benefit from the benefits enjoyed by the previous client.

A house may not sell, despite the best efforts of a home stager. Some properties have problems that deter prospective buyers.

Therefore, Passionate Advocates have to be really clear on what they offer. It's a delicate balancing act. If they're too hard-nosed about their limitations, they scare clients away. They'll come across as cold and indifferent.

Many business owners unconsciously find themselves marketing as Passionate Advocates without realizing what they're getting into. If you genuinely love your work and relate emotionally to your clients, it's easy to create marketing materials that promise far more than you want to deliver.

When you catch yourself sharing stories of your passion, and the times you went the extra mile, you may seem to be making the Passionate Advocate promise: "I'll do whatever it takes…"

Even worse, when your clients expect "above and beyond" service as non-negotiable, you know you might need to tighten the message.

Passionate Advocates combine passion with business.

They're not charities. They charge for their services and often charge a premium. They're not going to be confused with Mother Teresa and they won't help everyone.

Passionate Advocates have strong egos. They know they can help their clients and they're not afraid to say so. But they're also willing to say "no" when they know they can't be helpful.

Passionate Advocates market by establishing their authority and building trust. On the rare occasions a Passionate Advocate seeks my services, I often suggest they write a book or at least some op-ed columns. At the very least, their website should include colorful stories. Blogs work well for their marketing.

Passionate Advocates rarely maintain email lists. There's no need to build relationships because clients won't need them until they really, really need them. Urgently. Now. Maybe yesterday.

Very few people are interested in getting messages from DUI lawyers when they enjoy a clear driving record and avoid drinking too much at a party.

Passionate Advocates don't maintain mailing lists. They probably aren't reading this book. And then there's a category that almost certainly will not be reading this book. Celebrities have an audience that's begging to hear them. And they don't care what we write about them.

Chapter 9: The Celebrity

Many years ago, a business owner named Ali Brown shared a story about joining her family to care for a relative who'd been hospitalized. She moved the family members from their modest Best Western to the Four Seasons. The hotel treated them like royalty, even packing a lunch for them to take to the hospital.

Ali shared stories of buying her first house on the beach. Before she married and moved to Arizona, she shared stories of a night on the town in Los Angeles with her girlfriends. Her stories included small touches that added credibility, such as her decision to rent a limo to drive everyone to the different stops and made sure everyone got home safely.

Celebrities usually aren't actually celebrities, but Ali comes close. She has appeared on The Secret Millionaire, a short television series featuring millionaires who went undercover to explore charities and then donate $100,000. But most aren't known widely outside their industry.

Promise and Delivery

Celebrities make the promise, *"I am in a position to do what I like. I enjoy things that most people could never achieve. I will succeed even if I break the rules. Because I've achieved this level, I've earned the credibility to advise my clients."*

To make this brand work, you obviously have to have the lifestyle and make a credible claim that you earned this lifestyle through your business skills. You'll now mentor others who want to achieve the same success levels.

That's a Celebrity theme: being rewarded for their accomplishments and applying those rewards to help their families.

Celebrities tend to create very high-quality content. They're big on outsourcing so they'll have professional copywriting, design and photography. They hire copywriters and designers who help them send a strong message.

Celebrities communicate their promise by their appearance as well as their content. They might hire a stylist or casually mention their $400 haircuts. Some dress high-end designer styles and advise their followers to dress for success. Some wear wrinkled t-shirts and torn jeans.

When Celebrities share personal stories, their purpose differs from the Role Model. They position themselves as aspirational identities - someone their clients would like to *become.* Clients with more modest aspirations still enjoy reading about them, the way people enjoy reading juicy articles in *People* magazine.

Celebrity Superpower: Charisma

Celebrities command attention. They're the kids in the iconic American high school who were cheerleaders, football players, and prom queens. They're the legendary entrepreneurs who started in a garage and built an empire.

Celebrities always planned to play on a bigger stage, from the moment the ink dried on their business license. They wanted to be known and they wanted to be a little bit outrageous.

You might think of celebrities as "Loud and Proud." They're not always famous (although they're clearly hoping it will come). They might dress or speak in a style that sets them apart from their competitors and stir up controversy.

Celebrities build their audience's curiosity about themselves and their personal lives.

The Audience For Celebrities

Celebrities attract two kinds of followers.

First, brand-new business owners often look to celebrities simply because they're so visible. They make everything seem easy and fun. Their emails often share glimpses into a life most of us can only dream of. New business owners follow Celebrities the way people follow the British royal family, actors, or comedians.

Second, high-end businesses and entrepreneurs who want to play on a big stage also follow Celebrities. They're hoping to become Celebrities themselves.

For both these groups, Celebrities represent what sociologists call an aspirational reference group. Followers look up to them. They're fans and sometimes groupies.

A Celebrity email begins, "Check out my playlist...get ready to shake your booty and break out the martinis!"

She knows: her followers will be curious about what she's listening to. She makes a sly reference to "shake your booty." That's a Celebrity for you.

But don't be fooled. She's extremely smart. She delivers the goods.

Lorrie Morgan, a high-end copywriter, tells a different kind of lifestyle story.

Every email communication shares a story of Lorrie's life in the Arizona desert, where she keeps horses and rides daily. She maintains a lifestyle that a few would want to emulate and that many find fascinating. How is she welcoming a new horse who's afraid of people? How does she deal with a scary rattlesnake?

Mostly, she conveys her love of life, ability to triumph over obstacles, and openly relishing the rewards of being internationally recognized in her field.

Celebrities bask in the spotlight.

They're solo performers...standup comics, not members of an improv team. They're solo vocal artists, not choir members. Their sports would be baseball or golf, honoring individual players who can transform a team or who don't need a team. They love bringing in the home run while the stands fill with cheering crowds. They know how to bring out the capabilities in their clients and the people they hire. You'll rarely see them entering contests; they won't risk coming in second.

Celebrities know how to reach their fans on an emotional level. They understand they won't be universally loved; in fact, some of the most successful celebrities draw a response of, "I can't stand them" when their names come up. They don't care; they epitomize the image of laughing all the way to the bank.

They're quick to spot trends, especially contemporary slang and phrases that show they're "in." The women tend to follow fashion; men tend to be photographed in wrinkled t-shirts, looking like they forgot to shave.

The Celebrity makes the claim, "I've reached a great deal of success by my work and I am well-placed to help others because of what I've achieved." They don't feel shy about talking about money and being rewarded with money. You know you're talking to a Celebrity when you hear, "There's nothing wrong with being paid five thousand dollars for something that took you an hour, as long as you deliver value."

Celebrities view their clients as loyal fans. They carefully set boundaries and guard access. A one-to-one consulting session will be positioned as a reward, limited to their most special clients. Being "nice" is important to a Celebrity but being "approachable" isn't. There's often good reason for this choice: celebrities attract fans who can be greedy. As small businesses, they rarely hire security to protect them; they need to establish their own barriers.

You can't imagine meeting a Celebrity for lunch. Celebrities build their brand by maintaining a strict red velvet rope policy. They'll hold a big event, sell tickets, and let you reserve a place at their table... for a price.

Content: Celebrities write about themselves and they're not particularly modest.

One Celebrity sends emails with subject lines like, "I'm going away for a while," or, "I like to be different."

She writes about herself...

""I've jumped off a lot of cliffs in my life. Every leap has only led me back to myself. The reason why I was able to grow my company quickly (as in, hitting 7-figures one year after launching my first online course)."

"I've been described as an award-winner, a 7-figure business owner, a best-selling author..."

You get the idea. Clearly some people will be annoyed, dismissing these comments as self-centered and pompous.

But this business owner clearly has a strong following. I believe her when she says she's a 7-figure earner, and that's a very big deal... although I've also heard of 7-figure earners who went bankrupt with overspending.

Ultimately, Celebrities can be polarizing. Some people hate them... and they cry all the way to the bank.

Business Strategy: Celebrities go BIG.

They plan BIG events. While not all live event hosts are Celebrities, it's rare to find a Celebrity who hasn't hosted something live or at least a live stream.

Subject lines like "The responses have been overwhelming!" Anything with shock value ("How I almost died!") Anything with the word "pants" (as in "Stuck with picnic pants?" or "Put on your big girl pants" or "The day my pants fell off") Anything with "badass"

Pitfalls: Celebrities need to be able to deliver on their very strong promises. They're usually extremely talented as well as charismatic, so they readily draw clients who say, "I want to be like you."

As a marketing strategist, I often work with business owners who view a particular Celebrity as a mentor. This relationship always reminds me of the truism, "Good players don't always make good coaches - and vice versa."

What works for a Celebrity archetype won't work for business owners who are starting out or who simply resonate with a different message. Celebrities begin most content with a fascinating story about themselves. They can get away with writing about their latest adventure, which may have nothing to do with their business.

Other business owners need to begin by anticipating the question, "What's in it for me?" They share stories only in the context of lessons or examples for their clients.

Celebrities work hard but give the impression they're living a life of leisure. They often talk about how little they work, at least now. They work hard to sound humble, but they rarely do.

How do you know you're dealing with a Celebrity?

There's one dead giveaway. If you get an email signed "Hugs," "Love," or, "Warmly," or some variation of those closings, the odds are very high you are dealing with a business owner whose marketing is based on the Celebrity archetype.

She doesn't care. She doesn't think about archetypes. She's arrived.

Section 3:
Using the new style of branding.

Now that we've covered the archetypes and you're ready to brand, how do the archetypes work, anyway? That's a question I get consistently from clients.

In this section, you can see how other solopreneurs have used the 5 archetypes in their branding.

Most solopreneurs won't have heard of the archetypes, but I've been surprised at how many of the most successful have unconsciously adapted an archetype. When you review their marketing, it's obvious.

Once you've identified your archetype, you can make wise choices about branding, rebranding, stories, and even email marketing.

My most astonishing discovery was that solopreneurs consistently used the same forms of email signoff, depending on their archetype… and they did this even when they didn't consciously know their own archetype.

Innnovators signed off with, "Cheers" and Celebrities ended with hugs and kisses. And Role Models almost always include a reference to success: "To your success" or "To your sweet success."

Chapter 10: Strategic Choice #1: Choosing your archetype

Show me a successful business. I'll show you a business that has adopted an archetype—usually subconsciously. When we analyze their marketing, we realize their marketing consistently follows a pattern.

A successful business sends a consistent message. If your business is not successful, you are probably sending an inconsistent message. Understanding your archetype will help.

This chapter gives you an example of how you might review your options as you get ready to create content to support your positioning. We'll use an example of a small, service-based solopreneur type business.

Belinda's Story

Belinda started her business after taking several courses in improv theater. Originally she had taken those courses just to have fun and meet people.

Then, like so many solopreneurs, she made the connection between her hobby and her business dream. She wanted to bring the playful, spontaneous attitude of improv to corporate businesses. She named her business "The Playground" and she created a website about children's games: jungle gyms, hopscotch, and dodgeball.

Belinda had no trouble defining her mission statement.

"I help companies develop a creative culture. I show them that 'play' is not a four-letter word," she said.

At Belinda's request, I've changed her name and the details of her business. But many - perhaps most - business owners will see themselves in Belinda.

Belinda's Challenge

Belinda got ready for business by spending a small fortune on her website. On the advice of a well-meaning consultant, she spent lots of money creating an online storefront. Her site drew lots of "Wow!" reactions. But her visitors rarely turned into clients.

Belinda became even more frustrated when she attended networking events. Other business owners would ask, "What's your story?" and she'd freeze. When she talked about her business, people's eyes would glaze over. "Interesting," they said.

Belinda was going broke. She had to take drastic action.

Belinda's first step was to answer the classic copywriting question: "So what?"

Why do companies want to build creativity into their culture? Why do they want to be more playful?

"When a company - or division - becomes creative," Belinda explained, "they increase employee engagement. Employees become more productive. Teams finish their projects faster and resolve conflicts more quickly. And people stay around longer so you don't need to re-hire."

There are lots of consultants who help companies increase productivity and manage conflict. Belinda has developed a new way to do this - a unique program that's not available anywhere else. Most consultants do not have the training, interest or motivation to offer this program.

Belinda's second step was to choose her archetype, so her message and content would be consistent.

Here's what she considered.

Role Model

Although she was a solopreneur, she was targeting medium size companies that were focused on the bottom line. They wouldn't buy into, "If I did it, you can too."

Anyway, she had never done the things she recommended to her clients. She was like a sports coach who had never played a game.

Passionate Advocate

Theoretically, Belinda could position herself as a Passionate Advocate - the consultant who promises, "I'll go the extra mile to help. Whatever it takes!" She'd ride in like the cavalry and save the day.

The idea was appealing. She knew she was solving a big problem for companies. She felt a passionate devotion to her business. It was like a cause. She was ready to give her business everything she had: all her energy and emotion would pour out here.

However, Belinda recognized the two biggest challenges of Passionate Advocates: setting boundaries and creating unrealistic expectations. She didn't want clients calling her at 3 AM with a question or problem. She wasn't prepared to promise them miracles.

Besides, most of her clients didn't see themselves as desperately in need of an immediate solution. They knew they had a problem but it wasn't a matter of life or death of any person or business.

Celebrity

Belinda didn't feel ready to position herself as a Celebrity.

Solopreneurs who are Celebrities aren't usually featured in mainstream media. You won't see them on the Today show. They won't get featured in the *New York Times* magazine.

But Celebrities share that "I can do anything" swagger. They break rules. As I said, they wear unconventional clothes: anything from ripped jeans to sloppy t-shirts to designer outfits and $400 haircuts.

Many use language that could make a sailor blush and get them banned from G-rated programs.

This wasn't Belinda.

Maybe someday she could position herself this way, but now wasn't the time.

Educator

Ultimately, like many service-based business owners, the choice fell between Educator and Innovator archetypes.

Belinda could adopt the Educator archetype. After all, she'd always been a good student. She'd taught a few college courses. She enjoyed speaking and lecturing.

If she chose the Educator archetype, her marketing would focus on providing information through sharing content, webinars and presentations. She'd develop a blog with articles that would generate a lot of "aha" moments.

She'd send a weekly or monthly newsletter to corporate HR managers, offering tips and advice on corporate culture. She could even write a book or start a podcast.

A lot of her content would be straight-up education. A blog post might be, "A Team-Building Activity That's Better Than a Scavenger Hunt."

She might talk about a company that struggled to get new employees to work together. She'd give an example of a successful intervention - and then explained why it worked, possibly with reference to psychological principles.

There was nothing in the Educator archetype that contradicted Belinda's values.

Innovator

Belinda ultimately decided to position herself as an Innovator archetype. She promises to deliver a unique solution to a problem the clients are eager to solve. She emphasizes that others can't make the same promise: she has unique skills or software.

Most important, Belinda would tell stories showing how others had reached success by working with her. These stories are critical to Innovators, who by definition offer solutions that will be new to a skeptical market.

Like the Educator, she might talk about a successful intervention to bring employees together. Instead of focusing on why it worked, she'd explain why her unique program made it possible...and why competing options won't be as effective.

Once Belinda recognizes her archetype, her marketing action steps become clear.

Her clients will be corporate managers who have tried everything "everybody knows." So far nothing has worked. They're not desperate - but they are actively searching for ways to manage conflict and introduce creativity into their organizations.

Belinda's solution asks companies to take risks. They'll be trying out new activities - maybe some improv acting and team-building exercises–things they've never done before.

Newness can be scary so Innovators include "reduce the perceived risk" as a major component of their marketing.

Belinda's audience will wonder, "How do I tell the CFO that we're spending money on something playful? How can we get a left-brained engineer to bring a positive attitude to a workshop?"

She'll need to address these points in her website copy, her brochures, and her sales presentations. I'd advise her to write a research-based white paper as well. She's got to get buy-in from many people in the company. At least one will be a classic number-oriented left-brain who will ask, "Where's the evidence?"

Fortunately, Belinda has worked with a handful of clients who were thrilled with their results. She can ask permission to feature them in case studies; she might even make a video. Smart companies know a case study will be a win-win: they get publicity as well as a reputation for being bold and cutting-edge themselves.

Belinda needs a good story to support her brand.

Her story might be based on her own experience.

"I was studying acting and working a day job in tech. I was working with a team to implement a project that involved implementing new accounting software. It wasn't the type of topic that has you dancing on the tables.

"We had to work through a lot of details. We kept running into glitches so everything took longer than we expected. Our team started to fray at the edges. We had a few outright clashes and a couple of people actually stopped speaking to each other. Our boss sent someone from HR to do some team-building exercises. When she suggested a scavenger hunt, we all united in one big, 'NO!'

"I'd been studying improv and I got an idea. I asked if people would be willing to experiment with an exercise where we'd draw something on paper and then talk about it. To everyone's surprise, even the engineers and accountants agreed to participate. We took the afternoon and…well, we just played. Along the way we started laughing. People opened up about what they were worried about.

"The next day, we felt like a brand new team. People felt refreshed. They came up with breakthroughs. They talked…at least enough to be polite. Since then I turned the process into a repeatable system, and I work with clients to get the same results I experienced for the first time at that project."

If Belinda didn't have her own story, she could use a client's story. She could quote the client's CEO or VP-HR, or she could share the story entirely in the third person.

Either way, success stories are the bread-and-butter of Innovators.

If Belinda had chosen an Educator archetype, she'd find a different story. She'd find a metaphor to explain what she does and how it works. She might say, "This is like…"

From Story to Brand

As an Innovator, Belinda knew her website would need videos that demonstrated what she did. She'd need to have testimonials that specifically addressed her innovative approach.

And now her website practically wrote itself. She knew how she was unique. She understood what she wanted her clients to remember her — as someone who'd solved a problem no one else could. At the same time, she'd need to clarify what she offered and what the clients needed to bring to the table.

But she knew what she needed. She knew exactly where to direct her focus.

Can you have two archetypes?

Many clients say, "I seem to be a little bit of two archetypes."

Belinda might say, "I educate my clients when I market to them. After all, I have a blog and I may offer a podcast."

As an Educator, her content would focus on concepts. She'd dig a lot into the "why" behind the problem and her solution.

As an Innovator, her content supports her program. She'll probably decide she doesn't need a blog or podcast. Unlike an Educator, her credibility won't come from demonstrating her overall expertise. She won't be generating "aha" moments.

More likely, she'll sell her program with testimonials from happy clients. She'll create a free report with case studies. and Much of her content will be directed to her program. She can certainly create educational videos, blog posts and presentations. But they'll support her program 100%.

You'll gain maximum benefit from marketing with one archetype. You'll have ONE category of story.

You're not locked in.

As you grow your business, you might realize the archetype you chose no longer feels comfortable. Over time, your business may change.

Let's review Belinda's story. As she builds a clientele, she might find she's interviewed by major media. She develops a reputation. Her name commands respect and higher fees. From a marketing perspective, she becomes bolder–even a little outrageous. She begins to evolve toward the Celebrity archetype.

Alternatively, she might decide she wants to educate clients. She plays more of a consulting role. She might even start a training program - "The University of Creativity" - taking pains to establish that she's not passing herself off as a true academic institution.

She might also decide to play on a bigger stage. She's got an innovative idea that can be used by a range of businesses. Her story might get picked up by the media. She could become known as a personality and her clients now become raving fans.

Now she's a Celebrity archetype! She shares different stories. Now she'll talk more about her own life. She'll use stronger language. She'll show off her success

Chapter 11: Strategic Choice #2: Rebranding

If you stay in your small business 3 to 5 years, you will need to rebrand…or at least consider a rebrand.

So the question comes up…

"Do I need to rebrand my business? I'm exhausted just thinking of going back to looking at colors and type fonts...not to mention coming up with clever taglines."

Let's get this squared away.

First, this approach to branding refers to an outdated version of branding–one that may still work for big brands with a big advertising budget.

As a small business, you can't brand beer or cola drinks or sportswear. You're branding YOU. That means your message is more important than your colors or logo, and the best way to share your message is to tell a story.

As a small services business, you get your brand advantage by focusing on your story.

Second, very few people wake up and say, "I need a new brand." If you can relate to these 3 challenges, you might really be saying, "I need a brand."

(1) You're getting lots of leads and attention...but the wrong people are asking about your services. They take up a lot of time and they may be a lot of fun to talk to, but they're not your best clients.

(2) You keep getting asked to tell your story...at networking meetings, conversations with prospects, follow-ups to your speaking gigs. And you're not sure what story to tell. You're looking for a story that's fun to tell and (more important) conveys your value. Even worse, you might be telling a story that actually hurts you and your business. You're sending the wrong message.

(3) You're making a change in your audience. You've been doing the same thing for a long time. Sometimes this happens because you get an opportunity to swim in a bigger pond. Your clients are bigger, more knowledgeable, maybe more sophisticated

This rebranding happens because you began by marketing to low-hanging fruit. Or you get introduced to an opportunity that's potentially lucrative and lets you play on a bigger stage.

So if you're seriously rebranding, you begin with the question: "What's the best story for my new message?"

For example, a business owner I'll call Louise has been coaching creative artists and writers. She's always been part of that community. She positions herself as a creative who became successful and her message is, "I did it! So you can too!"

Now she gets invited to present a corporate workshop on creativity. She realizes she could target corporate executives who want to bring more creativity and joy into their lives. After some research, Louise realizes this corporate market could be quite lucrative. Her coach encourages her to begin a business pivot or (if you prefer) a new direction.

But her message has to change. She's never been a corporate executive. So, in the words of one of my own clients, "I need to market to people who are not like me!"

At first, Louise was overwhelmed. "I haven't walked in their shoes," she said. "My first business coach told me to market to people like myself. But in this case, I'm not marketing myself! Why would someone believe I can help them?"

Louise originally expected to continue her brand with the Role Model story archetype. Role Models brand their own experience with stories about their own struggles. Their message takes some form of, "I'm just like you. If I did this, you can too."

That archetype worked well for Louise when she targeted stay-at-home moms. But now she'd be relating differently to her new audience. For one thing, she'd never been a corporate executive.

So now she needed to change her message, which means changing her story.

Louise had a story that resonated with her audience of solopreneur creatives. She could share her experience of moving from a struggling solopreneur to a confident, profitable business owner. But she couldn't tell an origin story about moving from frustrated corporate executive to confident, fulfilled professional.

Her original "how I got started" story would most likely be irrelevant; she'd use stories to showcase her successes with clients. She might use stories to illustrate important points.

For rebranding you need these 3 stories. We'll illustrate with Louise's rebranding.

Story #1 - the new origin story you tell when you're asked, "Why did you make this shift?" In the early stages you'll need a connect-the-dots story.

Louise can't say, "I saw a way to make more money." She can say she started getting invited to help corporate executives. That's better.

Ideally, though, a story would be something like, "My background includes an MBA so I saw an opportunity to combine my skills."

Or, "From running my own business I was able to see how creative concepts would apply."

A senior bank executive once told a group, "I was an art history major in college. But I realized that I learned to recognize patterns and look at things in a new way."

In her book Generally Speaking[22], Claudia tells us that her philosophy major helped her become an effective intelligence officer and, later, a General in the US Army. Philosophy teaches you to think logically and make reasoned inferences.

Story #2 - the new success stories your new customers will share

Start out with some real ones as soon as possible, from your first clients. No clients? While you're in the planning stage, you can make up a story. You'll never present it as real. It's a story you use to plan your new business direction.

For example:

"When Eleanor and I began working together, she felt she had no life outside work. She didn't even own many casual clothes. She was feeling unfulfilled and could see she was heading for burnout. She was afraid if she took time off to do something creative, her work would suffer.

"We went through her schedule. Eleanor agreed to take a dance exercise class and a painting class every week for 6 weeks, and then evaluate. To her surprise, she actually performed better at work and began to receive complimentary thank you messages. She was even nominated for an award.

Eleanor has continued to grow. When I last heard from her, she had just received an unexpected promotion."

One caution: Make sure the outcome of this story will seem realistic.

A productivity coach wrote about working with a lawyer, a partner in a law firm. After making just a few changes, the coach's story concluded, "she had become chairman of her firm."

That's possible but not likely. Often the chairman of a law firm is a managing partner who's moving to retirement. It's a very different kind of role, not a natural progression. Anyone who knows law firms will raise a metaphorical eyebrow. The storyteller just lost credibility.

Story #3 will be a concept story - a metaphor that explains what you do.

"I'm like a personal trainer for executive women. You hire a personal trainer when you're feeling out of shape or when you want to reach new goals. Your personal trainer will review your current fitness levels and your goals. You'll get recommendations for things that seem far removed from exercise, such as diet and meditation. The goal is a high-energy, high-functioning fit body.

"I look at your life in the same way. What's missing? What's needed?"

So there you have it - 3 stories you'll need for rebranding your business. When you're ready to move in a new direction, no need to start with colors and slogans - begin with these stories.

And the 3 stories will be your connect the dots story, a concept story, and a success story.

Chapter 12:
Archetypes in Action: The Case for Email Branding

One of the ways the different archetypes market themselves: they use email as a branding tool. I'm sure none of the business owners I review had any idea they were following an archetype. But in reviewing their emails, the differences were obvious–and surprising.

Connie Ragen Green - the Role Model

The Role Model's message is, "If I can do it, you can too." She's just one step ahead of you on the path. She's so friendly and down to earth, her followers often feel they know her like an old friend.

She uses first names, so my emails look like this:

- *Cathy, open only if you believe in the power of video*
- *Cathy, she's returning today and I'll be there!*
- *Cathy, why you must experience the magic and power of live events*
- *Cathy, you could have knocked me over with a feather*
- *Cathy, could it be Santa driving down 5th avenue?*

These subject lines reinforce Connie's message. She's a mentor who relates to her clients like a more experienced friend -- the big sister who's a couple of years ahead of you. She reinforces the relationship with her content.

Incidentally, Connie continues this down-to-earth style in her sales copy. She's got a "Really Simple" series where she walks her audience through several marketing actions that normally would be considered quite complex. For one of her courses, at the time of this writing, her headline makes reference to apple pie, corn on the cob and summer bar-b-que.

Christina Hills - the Innovator

The Innovator brands on being able to solve an urgent problem by offering a one-of-a-kind solution . The message is, "These benefits are meaningful and you can't get them anywhere else."

Christina's innovation relates to the way she delivers her website creation course.

Christina reinforces her innovator role by showing she's on the cutting edge in her field (so she was an “early adopter” of the new Gutenberg Press version of Wordpress, even more when it came out.

She's got lots of examples of people who succeeded with her innovative approach. She uses the word "new" often.

- *the simple truth about building an online business*
- *a wellness coach gives up and creates her own website*
- *install the 'classic editor' plugin before Gutenberg comes out*

Ian Brodie - the Educator

Educators brand by being knowledgeable. Often they're positioned as authorities. They're not necessarily teachers in the traditional sense. They get the audience's attention - and claim credibility - by sharing lots of information. But they don't just present facts. They create lots of "aha moments.

Some of Ian's subject lines:

- *why don't clients buy from you?*
- *3 marketing secrets stolen from my local coffee shop*
- *my worst sales meeting ever*
- *how to lose a sale*
- *the simple secret of follow-up that works*
- *does 'just be yourself' lead to success?*

When Ian's describing something from his experience - such as his local coffee shop - the subject line shows that he's getting ready to illustrate a marketing point. He's not sharing more of his own life, the way a Role Model would.

One subject initially didn't seem to fit: *Sting vs Lady Gaga*. But it's actually a concept story -illustrating a key point that Ian wants to make about authenticity. Educators love concept stories. I drive my friends crazy with them.

You can learn more about concept stories through my Udemy course on marketing with stories and through my ebook on Amazon, Grow Your Business One Story at a Time.

Unnamed - the Celebrity

I decided not to name the business owner who adopted the Celebrity archetype (although you may recognize her if you're on her list). I don't know her so I'll seek permission first.

Celebrities brand by making the claim, "I've achieved great success and a great life through my work. That's my credential! And because I've been so successful and earned substantial rewards, I'm qualified to help you do the same.

This unnamed celebrity does exactly what I recommend for Celebrity archetypes. She's promising insider access and taking us behind the scenes. And she's referring to her lifestyle.

- *behind the scenes: how I built my social media biz*
- *the one mistake I hear a lot of solo-preneurs talking about*
- *we flew all the way to Mexico to hear this person*
- *my guest this week is a bad influence*
- *a behind the scenes look at my weight loss journey*

Email Openings

Getting subscribers to open their emails can be a challenge. Once opened, they need to be persuaded to keep reading.

Educator:

I'm back with another video marketing tip.

It was triggered by a discussion in our weekly Momentum Club Zoom call which highlighted a big gap in almost everyone's marketing plan.

This video tip shows you how to fix that "missing link" - and one of the best and easiest ways I've found to implement that fix.

Role Model:

Hi Cathy,

I woke up this morning thinking about the habits that have taken me to where I am in my life right now. Much of this has to do with my morning routine, so I quickly wrote down my thoughts and added them as the next message for my "Action Habits Challenge." This is some of what I shared...

Innovator:

You know how sometimes we try to do "all the things" and we get overwhelmed?

And we try to do it all because we're afraid of missing out on the magic trick that's going to shift everything for the better, right?

Yeah, I get that. ;-)

But after 15+ years coaching online business owners and running a (at least) 6+ figure business since 2009 myself, this is what I know for sure:It's not about the next-best-thing.

Celebrity:

What if there were a place you could learn new marketing skills as you need them? What if you could find out why the best performing firms grow faster and are more profitable?

We created X University for marketers and firm leaders like you. So you can get better results. Faster.

*Get a full month of X University for just $10—an incredible savings of $200!**

Cathy, only read this if you want consistency and profitability in your business.

Email Closings

If you're at all consistent with your marketing, your email signoff will be a dead giveaway for your archetype. It's mostly unconscious.

The Role Model signs off on her emails with some version of "To Your Success," It might be, "To Your Sweet Success," or, "To Your Amazing Success," or, "To Your Ongoing Success," Almost always, when you see an email with this signature, you know you're dealing with a Role Model.

Educators sign off with something like, "Until Next Time."

Innovators (for some mysterious reason) often sign off with "Cheers," British marketers also sign off with "Cheers," so it's not a reliable indicator.

Celebrity signoffs convey strong emotion. For example:

"Written with a Smile."

"Can't Freaking Wait."

"Hugs."

"Much Love."

A Celebrity who's a marketing coach may urge you to follow her example. Rarely a good idea!

HOW FREQUENTLY TO MAIL

When you're a small business owner who's marketing online, you build a relationship with your followers. One of the most effective ways to do this is by building a mailing list. Business owners who email every single day, 7 days a week. They even send out an occasional "bonus" as an extra.

I know equally successful business owners who send long emails weekly, twice a month, or even monthly. Still others send emails only when they have something to announce.

Your Story Archetype can help you decide how frequently to email. You maintain a consistent message as you respond to the expectation of their audiences.

Role Models typically send emails frequently. They're the ones who will tell you, "I've sent daily emails for the last five years and haven't missed a day."

Role Models base their brand on the promise, "I'm just like you. If I can do it, you can do it." They share personal details more than other archetypes (and the profitable ones instinctively know what to share and what to keep quiet about).

So they find great success by opening with a personal anecdote, which may be loosely related to the topic of their message. They may include a few friendly tips. They often promote a series of products. Their audience doesn't mind; they feel they're talking to an older friend or sibling who guides them to make wise choices.

Educators rarely send emails purely for promotion. Their promise is, "I've got knowledge that can help your business, should you choose to apply it." So you get at least a small dose of information packed into each message.

They make sure each message includes substantive information. They're the ones who send messages so detailed that each one could be an ebook. Alternatively, some send shorter messages more frequently, ideally containing an "aha" moment. You'll rarely hear from an Educator on a daily basis.

Innovators send emails when they're got something new to announce. They promise solutions to tough problems. They promote their own programs and sometimes work with affiliates (although in my experience, Innovators tend to be fussiest about choosing affiliate and joint venture partners).

Passionate Advocates rarely maintain email lists. They may try and realize it's a waste of time. They promise to "go the extra mile" and few people think about needing that kind of help unless they're in search mode.

Celebrities resemble Role Models, but they send bolder messages (often with headlines that startle and shock). They don't share everyday stories about weeding the garden; their followers admire what they do but rarely expect to emulate them.

One Celebrity wrote, "I like to spend most of my time in my den, eating steak, smoking cigars, and drinking single malt Scotch."

Notice the subtle references to high-end consumption patterns. It's aspirational, not relational. He's not a celebrity in the conventional sense (though well known in his field), but he's extremely successful and bold.

Maybe you're not meant to send daily emails.

After I noticed this pattern, I understood why I have always had trouble sending daily emails. It's exhausting to come up with tidbits of knowledge even 5 days a week.

One Educator I've followed (and admired) for years has experimented widely, settling on 2 days a week. I find that a reasonable goal for me is 2–3 emails weekly (and I resend to unopens as well).

I also admire the Educator who sends long, memorable messages weekly. When you send less frequently, you can go deeper. More than once, I've emailed her to express my appreciation for one of her ideas. So I may do some experimenting in the foreseeable future.

Sending a daily message brings benefits.

If you're experimenting, aiming for a daily email message would be a good way to start. Your followers become accustomed to consistency. You get in the habit of writing. You create content you can use later.

Emails from all archetypes include a call to action.

Regardless of archetype, business owners (especially small service-based businesses) realize that emails aren't written for fun.

Even those who write long, thoughtful messages include a call to action; some include several calls to action. They promote their lead magnets, affiliate products, tripwires, paid memberships, and more.

One Educator targets high-end clients with high-end offers. She doesn't just add calls to action; she has a "buy me a coffee" promotion on every message. She says it brings her success and doesn't detract from her message.

Regardless of your archetype, you can pick up email marketing tips from the experts. There's a lot of hype out there.

Chapter 13:
Conclusion: The Future of Small Business and Small Business Branding

Small businesses of the future will be operating in an increasingly competitive marketplace. Customers have more choices and more awareness of their choices.

Barriers to entry continue to be lowered as more services can be delivered remotely and as customers are demanding remote options. In the medical world, we're seeing patients demanding more remote telehealth options. Exercisers want in-home options. More and more companies prefer remote presentations rather than paying someone to travel for in-person meetings. Once a service can be offered remotely, the barriers to entry drop way down. We're seeing more solopreneurs in a world of "anyone can play."

At the same time, we're seeing motivation to become an entrepreneur for a wide variety of motives. Following the pandemic, many corporate workers realized they valued a lifestyle of freedom. So "anyone can play" becomes "everyone will play." We'll see a more competitive environment for small service businesses. Entrepreneurs - especially solopreneurs - will have to become smarter marketers.

What are the marketing challenges facing these small companies?

Credibility. Prospective clients look for signs of stability. Will you still be around? Can we know what we're getting when we sign up?

Communicating Value. Many smaller businesses offer services that didn't exist 20 years ago - some even 5 or 10 years ago.

Personality with Professionalism. Customers want to feel they're dealing with a real human being...but they don't want to get TMI and they don't want to sacrifice professionalism.

The archetype framework can help solopreneurs meet these challenges.

As of now, entrepreneurs get little guidance from courses and classes. Few of those classes identify the unique requirements of small service-based businesses. A lot of formal education gets delivered as "one size fits all." You get directives to tell stories without focusing on what stories are most likely to promote your brand.

Even more important, understanding your archetype can help you balance the personal with the professional.

Some people enjoy being "out there," warts and all, while some really want to be invisible. Some are proud of their weaknesses and want them on full display. Some marketing "experts" insist you have no choice: you have to share stories about your past and bare your soul.

When you understand your marketing style, you can recognize the degree of exposure - or lack of exposure - you'll be expected to share.

When you're a Role Model, you'll be "out there" far more than when you're an Educator or Innovator. When you're a Celebrity, you're on display and you manage your image.

So knowing the framework helps you manage your branding.You can decide how much - or how little - of that mess to put in your message.

End notes

Note: Because so much of this material comes from a living Internet, it is subject to sudden, unexpected change. People sell the names of their websites. Links can be removed with no warning. Everything was working when we went to press. We can't control what happens after!

Free quiz to determine your archetype.
Take the quiz cathygoodwin.com/archbook

Introduction:

1) US Chamber of Commerce:

www.uschamber.com/co/start/startup/what-is-solopreneur

Brene Brown

2) They cultivated stories: See my podcast interview with Cindy

Bidar

cathygoodwin.com/podcindy

Chapter 1:

3) Peter Hotez

journals.plos.org/plosbiology/article?id=10.1371/journal.pbio.3000024

Chapter 2:

4) Budweiser commercial

youtu.be/7p_3lITiK_Q?si=uKC0lwDBtTOOWhhi

5) Entrepreneurial Magazine: The Basics of Branding

entrepreneur.com/starting-a-business/business-the-basics-of-branding/77408i

6) Cadbury's gorilla ad:

www.youtube.com/watch?v=NHtEyDrD4oA

7) Contently.com explanation:

contently.com/2024/06/18/branding-moments-brand-storytelling-examples/

Chapter 3:

8) This Renegade Love:

thisrenegadelove.com/home

9) Jeep Renegade:

www.motor1.com/news/243112/jeep-renegade-refresh-spy-shots/

Jen Sincero - badass

10) Spirituality for BadAsses:

amazon.com/dp/B08SMP9982/

11) Tom Kuegler on Medium:

medium.com/blogging-mastery/your-writing-voice-doesnt-matter-focus-more-on-your-ideas-bb379ede714a

Chapter 4:

12) Pete Seeger's and Boxes on the Hillside:

youtu.be/I_FB9bwyp6M?si=nv0Fvk0_ioFovSLR

13) HBR article:

hbr.org/2019/09/the-dangers-of-categorical-thinking

14) Relocation website:

https://movinglady.com

15) Book on relocation - Making the Big Move

amazon.com/dp/173244000X

16) Book TEll to Win by Peter Gruber

amazon.com/dp/B003F3PK9K/

17) Christina Hills website:

creationworkshop.com

Chapter 6

18) Jagdish Sheth:

jagsheth.com/consumer-behavior/consumer-resistance-to-innovations-the-marketing-problem-and-its-solutions

Chapter 7

19) Tara McMullin's article:

taramcmullin.medium.com/parents-deserve-more-than-positive-thinking-6d26436638c9

Chapter 8

20) Criminal law firm:

goldsteinmehta.com/

21) Divorce coach:

www.divorcecoachformoms.com/

Chapter 11

22) Claudia Kennedy, Generally Speaking:

amazon.com/exec/obidos/ASINN/0446527939/

About the Author

Cathy Goodwin is a former marketing professor who earned her Ph.D. at UC Berkeley's Haas School of Business. She taught marketing for over 20 years before turning to the Internet.

Through her website, CathyGoodwin.com, she has helped dozens of clients revise their copy and implement a profitable strategy that increases sales. She works virtually with clients from all over the world.

She specializes in helping service-based solopreneurs develop marketing content that will differentiate them from the competition. They will attract more clients who immediately "get" what they do and why they're unique.

Cathy has lived all over North America, including Alaska and Canada. She now makes her home in Philadelphia with two rescue cats who refuse to share their stories. Her avocations include ceramic sculpture, standup comedy, all kinds of fitness, and a fanatical devotion to reading murder mysteries.

DEDICATED to the people whose stories I'm using in this book.They taught me and inspired me to create the archetypes

ACKNOWLEDGMENT to Corinne Q. (Lindy) Berger, who patiently reviewed the book in detail and provided editing. "You need this!" she said firmly and she was right

Additional books and resources

Free quiz to determine your archetype
Take the quiz cathygoodwin.com/archbook

Business Ebooks on Amazon:
Grow Your Business One Story At A Time
Intuitiion for Business and Careers
Non-Business Book (paperback and ebook)
When I Get Old I Plan To Be A Bitch
Making the Big Move: Relocation As A Life Transition
Your 21-Day Extreme Career Makeover

Cathy's author page on Amazon where you can see a complete list of books

Strategic Storytelling Podcast
https://StrategicStorytelling.show

Cathy's business website
Cathy's career website
Cathy's "living" website